HIGHWAYS
FOR LEARNING

AN INTRODUCTION TO
THE INTERNET
FOR SCHOOLS AND COLLEGES

D0994471

CONTENTS

PREFACE

There are times when technology seems to be outstripping comprehension and when it leaves most people confused – dimly perceiving its possibilities, but not fully understanding the implications for them and their lives. The usual metaphor for the electronic information age is a highway and yet the cover of this booklet, the Honduis world map 1630, suggests an earlier parallel with human endeavour: the voyages of discovery of the late fifteenth and sixteenth centuries. This was the first time that the true extent and nature of the world became apparent to the few explorers and when very hesitant lines of communication were being established around the entire globe across land and sea by the early voyages.

These days we take for granted the capacity of telephone lines and television signals to relay messages instantaneously around the world, but the ability of the computer to send and receive information across powerful networks is still only just being appreciated, particularly in education and training. The Internet, that vast number of inter-linking computer networks with its origin in the USA, is currently receiving considerable attention in the media and has become so prominent that it simply cannot be ignored. Hence this introductory book for those in schools and colleges who are in need of guidance and answers to some basic questions.

But – no matter how large the Internet has become, nor how many gigabytes of data it holds – it still offers us only a glimpse of the services that will be possible in the future over truly broadband networks. It is a mistake to think that the Internet equals 'the information superhighway' for, with the exception of SuperJANET in the UK, we simply do not yet have a fully operational open broadband network for education. But what we do have, for those with the right equipment and connectivity, is the global Internet running over narrowband and linking over 30,000 smaller computer networks all over the world. At the time of writing, over 30 million people use it to exchange messages, obtain information about every subject imaginable and to take part in discussion groups. *Highways for Learning* is a basic introduction for teachers, trainers, lecturers and managers to an enormous subject and, while there are some technical details, the overall emphasis is on how the Internet might be used in education.

At this stage, our knowledge of the true potential of wide area networking technologies for education is comparatively limited and much of the evidence of Internet usage in schools is drawn either from USA experience or from small projects with which NCET is involved in the UK. Before long, NCET expects to bring out more detailed guidance and publications in the communications area, particularly in the light of the recent speech by the Secretary of State, Gillian Shephard, at the BETT conference in January 1995 and the commitment she expressed to a consultation process and funded evaluations of suitable broadband projects. We are facing a fascinating and challenging future and I believe that the UK is well placed to take advantage of the exciting possibilities offered by communications technologies.

Jeff Morgan
Director – Electronic Communications
February 1995

HIGHWAYS FOR LEARNING ON THE INTERNET

This book is published in two forms, on paper and on the Internet, each exploiting the features of the medium. Copyright conditions apply to both versions.

On the Internet *Highways for Learning*
- can be saved to disk, edited and printed out
- interlinks information
- links to other sites and information
- is updated as the Internet changes
- involves readers: e-mail your comments to the NCET communications team.

You will find it at:
        http://ncet.csv.warwick.ac.uk/WWW/randd/
                highways/index.html

Why not compare the two versions?

WHAT IS THE INTERNET?

1

'The Net is possibly the largest store of information on this planet. Everybody can be part of it; it is one of the few places where race, creed, colour, gender, sexual preference do not prejudice people against others. All this through the magic of modern technology. Communication is the key. People talking to people. The Net isn't computers. That's just the way we access it. The Net is people helping each other in a world-wide community.'

From the winning entry in a BBC competition to describe the Internet
Simon Cooke, physics student at UMIST, Manchester

The Internet, commonly referred to as 'the Net', is the largest computer network in the world. It interlinks over 30,000 smaller networks operated by universities, research centres, government departments, non-profit and commercial organisations world-wide.

The Internet is growing – more networks are being connected to it at the rate of one every six minutes. There are nearly two million servers on the Net, and each can contain thousands of documents. It is estimated that there could be 125 million users world-wide within two years. At present (1995), information is usually free to users; it is the connection to the Internet (from £10 per month) and local telephone charges which have to be paid for. These relatively modest costs defeat distance: the cost of connecting to Japan, India, Germany or London is the same – thus opening up a world of information and communication.

What was once the playground of an academic, American, male, computing élite, now offers something for everyone. Each person sees it differently: for one it may be the largest library on the planet to browse and contribute materials to; for another the fastest and most reliable postal service in the world; for still others it is a way to meet friends, to discuss politics and music, to share views and to exchange help and support.

The Internet owes its existence to an unlikely source: the United States Department of Defense at the Pentagon. A network of computers called the ARPAnet was built in the 1970s. The successors to that network, five super-computers, formed the original spine of the Internet. The super-computers were set up in the 1980s by the American National Science Foundation; in order to encourage researchers to send in their programs to be worked on by the super-computers and then sent back. The military developed dynamic re-routing to make the links 'catastrophe-proof'. This was done so that in event of an attack on part of the network, messages could be auto-matically re-routed via other links. The protocol that was designed to enable this routing was the 'Internet Protocol'. Today the Internet provides a means of global e-mail (electronic mail), file transfer and a vast world-wide information resource. Ironically, during the Gulf War the Americans were unable to destroy Iraq's communications systems because the Iraqis were using the Internet.

To begin with, most Internet users were computer enthusiasts in American universities and research centres. Increasingly, however, users are a more representative cross-section of people who realise that there is information to be had, thoughts to be shared, people to be talked to, and topics to be researched and disseminated. The gener-osity with which some ideas and materials are shared displays a magnanimity and open-handedness that it is hoped will endure.

WHAT WILL YOU FIND ON THE INTERNET?

You will find almost everything on the Internet. It is the 21st century version of an 18th century French project born of the optimism of the Age of Enlightenment: to create a single encyclopaedia of everything known by mankind. The French were defeated by the sheer growth of information and by the lack of technology to store and access it. As we approach the 21st century, however, the Internet could be that encyclopedia – and much more.

INFORMATION

The Internet brings information to people that they could find no other way through the World Wide Web. It provides access to more information than a librarian could dream of, all of which you can load into your own computer. Every ten weeks the number of computers providing information on the World Wide Web doubles. You can use the Web to visit museums, art galleries, libraries and exhibitions, even the White House and soon concerts, all for the cost of a local phone call. You can access the Library of Congress, science resources, journals, book reviews, business statistics, geological survey maps, United Nations papers, music, French language press reviews, software archives, sport databases, magazine archives. You can obtain weather details for most of the globe, images of outer space; the Bible is there, all the novels of Mark Twain, the plays of Shakespeare, the scripts of Blackadder. You can drop in on people's lives and homes. The pictures, text, data, video and audio files can be copied and saved for your own use (subject to copyright).

ELECTRONIC MAIL

E-mail is the most widely used facility on the Internet. Fast, cheap and efficient, e-mail on the Net is not just text: you can send and receive graphics and multimedia files as well and even set up video-conferencing links. It is easier and more cost-effective to send an Internet message than a letter or fax – just type your message and the address, click a button to send it and within seconds it arrives at its destination. Replies are even simpler on some computers – click a reply button, write your message, and it is automatically addressed and sent back. Messages can be stored and edited electronically. That is why the US postal service expects to lose 50% of its business to e-mail within five years. Before the Internet you could communicate only with subscribers to the same service, for example Campus 2000. Now, just as with the telephone (and the Internet Phone has just been announced), everyone with a connection to the Internet has a unique address and can exchange mail with any other Internet user in the world or indeed with large numbers of users: you can easily set up your own mailgroups.

DISCUSSION GROUPS

Usenet is a collection of some 12,000 discussion groups, the majority of which are useful and interesting (at least to those joining in them), although a few give the whole of Usenet a bad name. You simply find the name of a discussion group (sometimes called a newsgroup) and join it. You can then read the series of contributions, join in with your own ideas, comments or requests for help, or simply eavesdrop. For education there are groups for different subject areas and debates on current issues and two UK teachers' discussion groups have been established:

```
uk.education.teachers
uk.education.misc
```

Post your plea for ideas for lessons on a noticeboard and get a feel for the mutual help possible in the 'on-line staffroom'. With so many people out there in 'virtual communities', there is sure to be someone with the answer to your problem and who shares your interest in, for example, Star Trek, cats or music.

PUBLISHING

The Internet is changing the concept of publishing and new computer systems are being supplied with this in mind. Products like Microsoft's Windows NT server allow users quickly and easily to set up an Internet server: you can publish your own information – whether prospectus, article, poem, music or thesis – at low cost. Writers are now publishing manuals and fiction on the Internet; for instance, the Women Writers Project aims to make available on the Internet out-of-print or overlooked works by women. Project Gutenberg, based in Illinois, is publishing 10,000 literary texts on the Net, including Shakespeare, Tolstoy and modern texts and expects to give away millions of these annually by the year 2001. Most book publishers are setting up Web servers. Contrary to what you might think, sales of books tend to rise when they are published on the Net as well: it is still the case that a well produced book will win over a printout. Just as there was an explosion of books after the invention of the printing press, we can expect an explosion of digital books on the Net; the low cost and huge audience prove irresistible to anyone with something to say.

WHAT DO PEOPLE DO ON THE INTERNET?

Most Internet subscribers use the e-mail features and the World Wide Web. Here are two examples of how people could be using the Internet for education.

Jonathan, 13, is working at home on an assignment entitled For or Against Zoos. At school his class debated the issues and his teacher outlined the task to be completed in three weeks: to produce a leaflet setting out the arguments. Using his computer Jonathan had sent faxes to a number of zoos and animal welfare organisations and received leaflets from them within two days. He has a subscription to the BBC Networking Club which gives his family access to the Internet and connects to an animal rights discussion group with contributions from around the world. He browses through this, copying contributions and pasting them into a word processor. He then uses the Internet to 'visit' a zoo where he collects some images of animals and finds an on-line encyclopaedia with a section on the history of zoos. Using the word processor he assembles his ideas, edits the discussion statements and incorporates the historical item. Later he loads a leaflet template into a desktop publishing package, imports the edited text and adds the pictures. An hour later he prints out his leaflet.

The History

The first known zoo was set up by Queen Hatsleepsut of Eygpt at around 1500BC. 500 years later emperor Wen Wang founded the garden of intelligence, an enormous zoo that covered about 1,500 acres. Between 1000 and 400BC rulers of northern Africa, China, and India established many small zoos. These zoos were not for the animals but to display the wealth and power of the leader or ruler.

In ancient Greece public zoos were established so the people could come to study the animal and plant life. Students visited the zoo as part of their education. The Romans had many collections of wild animals for the bloody fights in the colosseum. During the middle ages, from around 400 to 1500AD zoos became very rare in Europe. At this time the world's largest zoo was still in China.

By the late 1400's people became involved in global exploration which made the Europeans want to have zoos once again. Explorers brought back strange creatures from the new world. These adventures found more than just animals. In 1519, the Spaniards discoverd a huge zoo built by the Aztecs in what is now Mexico.

During the next 250 years zoos were beginning to be built in Europe. Some of these only contained a few lions, tigers and bears, these zoos were called menageries. The animals were kept in small cages or pits behind iron bars. People began to think that menageries were cruel and refused to visit them. Through the years menageries were replaced by larger zoos where the animals received better care. These larger zoos became institutions for research as well as showing the animals to the public.

Some of these largers zoos are still in use today, the oldest of these is in Vienna, Austria. The Schohbrunn Zoo opened in 1752.

In 1907 a German animal dealer, Karl Hagenbeck, developed a new way of showing animals. He devised the moat technique. A moat of water or just a ditch surrouned the animals so the actual island in the middle was the same height as the public watching them.

By the 1960s zoologists realized that zoo could help save animals from extinction. They began to develop breeding programes. Before this many zoos had only one or two of each species. Few zoos owned more than one animal of a rare species. Today to make rare species less endangered and to create breeding herds, many zoos own several animals of one species.

Behind the Bars

Stating the facts about Zoos

Next year the school plans to set up its own Web server with contributions from students like Jonathan.

Pauline, who teaches at a college, is looking for some classroom ideas for her maths team over the coming year, particularly statistics and graphs. Her college network is connected to the Internet and she connects to the maths interest group on UseNet to see if there are any relevant discussion groups and picks up a few ideas posted up by a group of teachers in Scotland, pasting them into a word processor. She left an appeal for ideas for teaching notions of probability, hoping for some replies over the coming weeks, and then connected to Lycos, a Web Server which indexes information available over the Internet. Typing in keywords like mathematics, education and post-compulsory, she was led to 25 sites with relevant information. Not only did she find some detailed and practical ideas of immediate use, she also discovered the e-mail address of a teacher in Illinois who wanted to exchange questionnaire data with similar students, added to her personal hotlist of addresses of sites around the world to which she would return to discover more stimulating ideas and leads, and found a conference about motivating reluctant learners where someone had mentioned how useful the national lottery had been for developing notions of probability.

ETHICAL CONSIDERATIONS

The Internet gives people access to a wide range of material, a tiny amount of which is violent, inflammatory or obscene. The two most popular discussion groups are pornographic with one million visitors in September 1994. Most instances of unauthorised access to computers (hacking) have occurred via the Internet and computer viruses can be spread on it. In addition, copyright laws apply to Internet publishing as to any other form of publishing, but enforcement is difficult.

This negative side of a free, unregulated computer network is compounded in part by the ease with which digital information can be stored and exchanged. Material found on the Internet can easily be saved onto disk and distributed among friends. One disk looks identical to another and is easily slipped into a pocket in the playground. Publishing on the Internet is cheaper and easier than in the conven-

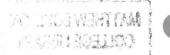

tional way; original material only has to exist in the form of a file on an Internet server for it to be read or copied by anyone on the network. The checks, balances, restraints and laws of the commercial world of publishing do not exist – but this is changing: an American has been imprisoned for what he published on the Net.

Undesirable material of whatever type is not as immediately apparent on the Internet, particularly on the Web, as it would be, say, to someone browsing in a newsagent's. A determined search will find some, but to students who use the Internet it will not be obvious: they are unlikely to meet it inadvertently. However, the fact that schools are legally required by law to act *in loco parentis* to under-16s has to be an overriding consideration and caution is essential.

What can you do?

- Be vigilant: make it clear to students that you know what they might try to do and have systems for tracking who uses each computer and which files they use.
- Let students know that unauthorised use of equipment and failure to follow the rules of the institution (eg loading and saving material onto disks from outside the institution) carry severe sanctions.
- Consider providing different levels of access, beginning with controlled access to information previewed by a member of staff, then e-mail and supervised open access to total open access.
- Although it may be difficult to prevent all unauthorised access, it is possible to prevent students accidentally discovering undesirable materials or messages through a combination of software and passwords – ask service providers for advice.
- Deal with criminal offences (obscene publications, unlawful copying) involving computers in the same way as you would with any other crime: involve the police.

Some service providers offer closed services without full Internet access, selecting suitable materials to save teachers time and preventing access to other material. Critics point that this may not be a com-

plete solution: access to e-mail and file transfer software means that determined students may be able to download unsuitable materials once they track down an address. Other companies are developing firewalls, solutions to monitor individuals' use of the Internet and improved local area network management systems which provide restricted access to Internet servers, as determined by the institution. Firefox, for example, are working on Nov*ix for Internet, enabling users of NetWare-based systems to restrict the services available to students. Microsoft are developing a 'server detective' to give network administrators monitoring tools to track how programs and applications are being used by each computer on the network. The system management server will be able to identify what and who has accessed certain sorts of files, eg pirated software.

NCET has produced a free leaflet about computers, pornography and the law – Computer Pornography, an Information Sheet for Schools – and IT centres run courses on tackling pornography and hacking.

GETTING ONTO THE INTERNET – FIRST STEPS

There are different ways of connecting to the Internet – via telephone lines, high-speed academic networks or cable – and there are different ways of paying for the access. These are covered in more detail in Chapter 3. Here, let us assume you are using a telephone line and a stand-alone computer.

1 Take advice and ask for personal recommendations. Decide whether your need is for e-mail only or full Internet access, including the World Wide Web. Talk to someone already using the Internet and take advantage of their experience. IT centres should be able to help.

2 You will need a computer which can:
   - be connected to a modem
   - run communications software
   - store and display graphics and large files.

8

As so often, the faster the computer, the more it is multimedia-ready and the higher its storage capacity, the better. But you can connect to the Internet at a basic level from surprisingly humble machines, in text-only black-and-white modes.

3 You need a relatively fast modem. At the present time a speed of 14,400 baud (= bits per second, ie about 200 words/second) is usual. They cost about £120 and often include fax facilities. However, 28,800 baud modems, twice as fast, are becoming affordable (under £400) and will soon be the norm. You can use a lower speed modem but you will spend more time on-line and most material will be tedious to access.

4 Take out a subscription to an Internet service provider, preferably for a short trial period rather than a full year. Depending on the level of service, the provider will give you an Internet connection, useful software, mailbox facilities and telephone and on-line help. Most require you to pay a subscription charge from about £10 per month, and some may impose a joining fee and connection time charges. See Appendix A for a list of service providers.

Competition between providers is increasing, tariffs and facilities often change and new service providers appear regularly. When choosing a provider these are some of the questions you should ask:

● Can I connect to the service at local call rate?
● How many modems per user does the service support? (15:1 is good.)
● How much will a year's use cost? (Include any initial registration costs, monthly subscription, on-line charges levied by the provider and the usual Mercury or BT call charges.)
● Are there additional time charges?
● Is it a service that caters for education?
● Is helpline support available? If so, is it there when needed?
● Does the service provide me with an Internet e-mail address?
● Does it provide full access to the Internet, or to e-mail only?
● How fast is access by 28,800 baud modem, leased line, ISDN?
● Is there user-friendly software for my computer?
● Is it easy to get started?
● Is documentation provided and is it of good quality?

Most of the providers describe how to access the Internet from PC-compatible and Apple computers. The software that has been developed world-wide is for those platforms. For Acorn computers, contact Acorn 01223 254254 for details of their Net application, Intertalk.

Welcome to the Natural History Museum's World-Wide-Web Server

This server is being developed to provide information on the Museum's exhibitions and public programmes and to provide access to information about the Museum's work and its collections.

If you are unfamiliar with HyperText and would like to know more about it click here (or press RETURN if you are using a character-based client).

The Natural History Museum is dedicated to furthering the understanding of the natural world through its unrivalled collections, its world class exhibitions and education, and through its internationally significant programme of scientific research.

The Natural History Museum's World Wide Web Home Page

THE INTERNET AND THE CURRICULUM

'Children have the most at stake regarding new media, since they will be around the longest. They are also most attuned to the potential of new media, because they are growing up with computers and other forms of information technologies.'

John Sculley, Chief Executive of Apple

The Internet itself, like paper or a CD-ROM, is a carrier of information and what it carries in 1995 does not yet provide resources tailored to the specific needs of UK teachers and learners. This chapter provides a snapshot (taken in early 1995) of ways in which the Internet is being used and sketches how the Internet might be developed to support the principal subjects in the curriculum.

Appendix D is a directory of Internet addresses which have been found to be useful in UK schools and colleges. These addresses will change and there will be additions. To get the latest information, go to the NCET server once you have established yourself on the Net:

```
http://ncet.csv.warwick.ac.uk/WWW/randd/
highways/index.html
```

Here, there are 'hotlinks' directly from the text to many of the sites mentioned.

The following sections contain sources of information, examples of current activities using communications technologies and speculation about potential future use related to the subjects of the UK national curriculum for ages five to 16. The chapter concludes with a section on information skills.

ENGLISH

At the moment the Internet is largely a world of words. English is the pre-eminent language of the Internet, even though many people will be using it as their second language. Accuracy, clarity, good spelling and correct punctuation are important for effective electronic communication, and use of the Net heightens the awareness of audience. Interpreting and summarising skills are needed to handle texts and messages received from a range of sources. For speaking and listening, classroom work in preparation for or arising from use of communication technologies provides many opportunities for developing speaking and listening skills, negotiation, discussion, persuasion and fluency. This is an area that English teachers cannot afford to neglect.

The Internet is attracting more and more publishers. The *Guardian* and the *Electronic Telegraph* are both on-line; film companies have set up Web servers for Disney films containing synopses and video clips; and there is poetry at Carnegie Mellon University. The Gutenberg server contains 2000 out-of-copyright texts, or, if you prefer, it is easy to download scripts of comedy shows like Blackadder. The Purdue On-Line Writing Lab Web Server offers a variety of writing-related information in an interesting and attractive format, lists of writing material on the Internet, other Writing Labs on the Internet and places to start your Internet-based research. The UK Office for Library and Information Networking is a directory of library services set up by Bath University.

The Internet provides a new audience

The English language will be developed through its use on the Internet (indeed, many argue that its world dominance will increase because of this), creating an important area of study and a means of gathering information about language variety and language use across English-speaking countries. Students will probably soon be using virtual multimedia libraries, providing new opportunities for them to conduct literary investigations. They will be using sophisticated information-handling skills to select, evaluate, edit and present information. For instance, multimedia texts could be imported, analysed, annotated and searched for themes. A Libraries of the Future project has been set up by NCET, with funding from the British Library and the Department of Education Northern Ireland, to develop visions of future libraries based on UK schools' experiences with the Internet.

Students will be collaboratively exchanging, reviewing, refining and publishing their multimedia work, and we may soon see 'organic' texts, existing only on the Internet, owned by no one, created by many, always readable but never finished. Mixed media texts may emerge with fixed sections on CD-ROM or paper, and dynamic, evolving text on the Internet. Services like 'Writers in Residence' will grow, as will collaborative writing projects enabling students to work with each other and with professional writers across the world. Support materials and discussion groups will emerge to help students with set texts (already the BBC is supporting *The Ancient Mariner* for GCSE in this way). Textbook, media and courseware publishers will exploit new markets in this area, and there are opportunities for professional associations and teacher education institutions to provide curriculum support for teachers.

MATHEMATICS

Communications technologies provide students with opportunities for using and applying mathematics in the solution of problems, helping to develop mathematical reasoning, and enriching work with number, shape, space and measures. In the area of handling data, in which students establish lines of enquiry and collect, analyse and interpret data, the Net can be particularly useful.

In the USA, Mathclub is an Internet-based educational service providing discussion groups for teachers and projects to help students explore on-line mathematics problems such as the notion of infinity. Like the MegaMath project, it is often oriented towards what in the UK would be called extension work for gifted students. The Shell Centre for Mathematical Education has its own Web server and you can visit a Gallery of Interactive On-Line Geometry. A Global Math

Research Project set up by a school in Australia asks classes to gather data on height and weight in a structured and consistent form (including standardised ranges and frequency counts) and then to send it for exchange with schools in other countries, analysing the data and discussing conclusions. In the UK a maths project involved the exchange of information on pupil sizes and body measurements with a school in Illinois, leading to analysis and discussions of the data. Mathematics teachers in Columbia USA shared their ideas on classroom teaching of times tables by posting them on the Internet after an in-service weekend.

It is likely that e-mail access to mathematicians in universities – 'Ask an Expert' schemes – would prove to be extremely popular with schools (and not just for mathematics). There is also scope here for accessing expert help with homework and for linking gifted students over the Internet to work collaboratively. As more data becomes accessible from servers, much of it will be useful raw materials for 'maths for real' projects – for example, plotting the progress of Antarctic voyages, the spread of lava from a volcano or, more prosaically, obtaining spreadsheet files of payment methods for buying a new car.

SCIENCE

Experimental and investigative science involves accessing raw data and obtaining evidence. In the study of life and living processes, students need to obtain information about health, to contact information sources such as zoos and museums, and to compare surveys of locally found animals and plants. In the area of materials and their properties, students' work is enhanced if they can communicate results and compare them with others'. In the area of physical processes, there are opportunities to study the application of science by following first-hand reports from around the world and to discuss scientific controversies.

Members of the academic science community are major users of the Internet. Many science journals are available on-line and are easy to download. For students there is the feeling of being part of a large community engaged in a worthwhile pursuit when they take part in, for example, the NetSpace Project.

Science on the Net is an area where generosity is especially noticeable. The NASA archives are there, as are the archives of the European space programme. The University of Florida makes available an on-line issue of *The Scientist*. Some of Stephen Hawking's original work is available from the University of Illinois. There is plenty on the Net for the biologist – even a Biologist's Guide to Internet Resources. Botanical resources are available from the Smithsonian Institute.

Using graphical Internet browsers like Mosaic, World Wide Web servers such as the Exploratorium in San Francisco, CERN in Geneva, Sea World and Busch Gardens, the Natural History Museum in London, the Smithsonian natural history collection and NASA can be reached and the contents downloaded. The information at NASA includes photographs of space from the Hubble telescope which can be stored and printed out for discussion in class. Two Web sites are currently vying for your attention in order to introduce you to the intricacies of frog dissection – one concentrates on the bits of the frog, the other on the actual operation.

The Corallia project enables students to follow on-line a survey of the ecosystem of a coral reef, examining the role of plankton and receiving daily atmospheric and oceanographic data from the survey ship. In future, students will follow scientific surveys as they happen, sharing in the surprises and excitement, making hypotheses and analysing data in real time. They will even be able remotely to control machines and cameras to obtain data.

Scientists will continue to exploit the immediacy of the Net and perhaps schools will develop links with higher education to enable school students to work with academic scientists. The are plans for a European resource bank to be set up containing a bank of videos of experiments with audio and text commentaries and activities. Conferences could be held on scientific topics, with papers, reports, contributions from around the world, followed by debates. The Japanese envisage expert (and highly-paid) teachers giving multimedia lessons / master classes – in science, for example – over networks to thousands of students.

In-service training schemes developed from projects like the Northamptonshire Distance Inset Project (details from NCET enquiry desk) will enable teachers to update their scientific knowledge and teaching skills with electronic links to each other, tutors and experts; these links could also be made available to students, enabling them to access rich external science resources and to question experts.

DESIGN AND TECHNOLOGY

It is important that students develop design and make skills and the associated ability to plan and evaluate. The wealth of material available on the Internet can act as an enormous visual resource for the teacher, allowing access to images of almost anything. The ability to download images from servers such as NASA acts as a starting point for design activities such as aerodynamic design, modelling and simulation. Food and nutrition students can exchange recipes and information about local dietary habits and cuisine.

Intertech Europe is a project involving schools in the UK and Europe on design topics. The students use communications technologies to co-ordinate and exchange work, and to plan and evaluate ideas. De-Zines is an Internet project to bring together design schools in Europe and the USA to work collaboratively.

In design offices across the world, staff routinely exchange plans and comments using communications technologies. Students will have access to the archives of companies and design centres, showing the stages from design to realisation of projects. They could establish links to firms anywhere in the world and take part in virtual work experience, with companies making use of young people's ideas and comments.

Resource banks of pictures and cross-sections of manufactured objects will develop which students can download and modify using CAD software. There could be world-wide competitions to design and make products, with UK schools working in partnership with others abroad, and consultants offering on-line comments and suggestions.

MODERN LANGUAGES

All aspects of the modern language curriculum are enhanced when students have access to communications technologies. It is essential that students are exposed to the target language and are given tasks which encourage purposeful and authentic use of the language.

Projects with Campus 2000 have demonstrated how modern language learning can be enhanced by communications technologies, and particularly e-mail. The key factors seem to be increased motivation via contact with real students in other countries and access to authentic language as a medium for achieving a common project task. UK schools regularly contribute foreign language items to Newsdays. The Goethe Institute runs 'Ask an Expert' days; the questions and answers have been edited and are now accessible on a database.

The French Télétel service (running at 1200 baud and already used by UK schools through Campus 2000) has 26 million users and holds vast amounts of information about all aspects of French life. In France you can see the type of on-line services developed when there is large-scale day-to-day home and workplace access. For example, about one in three TV advertisements end with a Télétel number for consumers to find out more and even order products on-line. It is only a matter of time before Télétel will be available over the Internet. Cities such as Paris, Grenoble and Marseilles and bodies like the French Ministry of Culture already have servers on the Internet, as well as on Télétel, with multimedia information relevant to the UK national curriculum, eg the environment, the local area, quality of life, shops and services, travel, culture and leisure.

The Human Languages Page on the Internet pulls together potentially useful language services like tutoring, sound samples of languages, on-line translation, dictionaries, resource banks and expert help. The Usenet news groups have sections on subjects such as the culture of Pakistan, Vietnam, the politics of China and Indian culture. On the same conference are opportunities to communicate with native French, German, Spanish and Russian speakers. Electronic mail and conferencing will certainly be one of the major Internet activities for language students – the feeling of the global village where barriers to communication such as cost and travel are suddenly removed is one of the first aspects of the Internet to strike newcomers.

There are increasing numbers of foreign language servers on the Internet accessible via 'sensitive maps' of sites in each country. They provide useful, relevant and topical information which just happens to be in another language – ie linguistic competence develops as a by-product. By its nature, the Internet will bring people speaking different languages into closer contact. By exchanging information with students in other countries, students will demonstrate increasing independence in language use, vary language according to audience and use language for real purposes.

Students will take part in conversations and conferences with native speakers over networks, using video- and audio-conferencing as well as text; exchange visits can be reinforced with preparatory and follow-up Internet links and there are predictions of virtual exchanges and 'telepresence' (it is already possible to visit 'digital Amsterdam' on the Internet). Increasingly we shall see automatic on-line translation of messages and other text, and students will need to spot nuances of meaning by referring to both original and translation. Digital radio on the Internet is set to expand beyond the current provision of one French language station, and decompression and file transfer will make receiving programmes a simple matter. In the future, the Internet could provide teachers and learners with ready-to-use banks of multimedia resources: a wealth of video and audio recordings from all over the world, transcripts (where the text matters more than its presentation, and so could quickly be printed off) and activities – all topical, fresh and, one hopes, setting high standards for methodology. We shall no doubt see providers of information and training for language teachers using the Internet to publicise events, courses, materials and services and even to provide a subscription-based remote training, advice and information service. A European project to explore some of these ideas begins in 1995 – for details, contact NCET.

HISTORY

The use of IT in history offers opportunities for students to use communications technologies to develop an awareness of the past and of chronology, to evaluate and use sources of information and to construct accounts of historical events and developments. Henry VIII is now on-line in Oldham via the Kidsphere initiative and inviting students to send him letters and ask questions about his life. Classes studying the Tudors and Stuarts within the UK national curriculum decide questions to put to the virtual king.

The low cost of publishing on the Internet will mean that archives will be open to the public – resource banks of primary source materials including maps, charts and historical documents – all reproduced to high standards of resolution. There are already many historical archives on the Internet in countries around the world such as that at the University of Florida which has an on-line exhibition with testimony, descriptions and first-hand accounts of the Holocaust. The Hellenic Civilisation database is a World Wide Web site in Athens with a wealth of textual and graphical historical information which can be downloaded and stored to disk for subsequent use in class by teachers or by older, more confident students who are researching for themselves. Students can make virtual tours of sites like Pompeii and visit exhibitions, such as 1492, which is at the Library of Congress. They can also follow the progress of an archaeological dig in Cambridgeshire.

Multimedia technology will make it possible to revisit historical periods and events. Conferences taking place over several months on themes such as the 50th anniversary of the United Nations (led by the University of Ulster) will develop.

Memories is an on-line witness project, where students can send messages to people who lived during the Second World War, such as A Land Girl, A Berlin Schoolboy and An American Soldier. Since the Internet defeats distance, we may see active retired people acting as on-line witnesses for local history. Indeed the Internet may turn out to be the key to a new lease of life, providing an outlet for the energies and experience of the retired in other ways too, such as giving individual help for students' basic skills in exchange for opportunities for further study on other areas.

GEOGRAPHY

The geography curriculum should provide opportunities for students to study places and themes, develop geographical skills, examine land use, environmental management and protection and to study weather and climate, transport, economic activities, population and settlements. Most of these areas can be enhanced with the Internet.

The BBC World Wide Web server provides hotlinks to Japanese servers in support of its Japan 2000 programmes and is well worth looking at for ideas for geography teaching (and other subjects). There are growing numbers of Internet servers (including the CIA) providing country-by-country information; the US census is one example, and it carries no surcharge. Weather is an important topic in the geography curriculum. Using the Internet it is possible to obtain from the universities of Edinburgh or Nottingham live weather data in the form of evolving satellite images which can be stored, studied and printed out.

In collaborative projects with schools in other countries, students exchange data about place for comparative purposes with students actually living in another place and climate. Some Internet servers, particularly in the USA, have relief maps which can be downloaded, along with topological data, for land use and geological surveys. In addition there are competitions (eg identify the city) and 'geo-trails' on the Internet.

Within a few years, schools could take part in collaborative projects to exchange information about contrasting areas. Virtual field trips to previously inaccessible places around the world are a distinct possibility. On-line conferences about geographical topics like human influences on desert formation could enable students to prepare and submit evidence and opinions. We may see on-line simulations on themes such as transport and settlements, making use of geographical information systems.

There is also a case for providing a bank of multimedia illustrations of geomorphological and settlement processes, such as river valley formation, coastal erosion and inner city land use, for schools unable to provide first-hand experiences on field visits.

ART

The art curriculum involves investigating and making, in addition to knowledge and understanding. Students are expected to record responses (using art vocabulary); gather and use source materials; keep a sketchbook to collect visual evidence and information to sustain a chosen idea or theme; respond to and discriminate between works of art; and compare art, craft and design across time and place.

The Net gives access to some of the best galleries in the world. The Hellenic Civilisation site has many photographs of classical paintings, sculpture and pottery in Greek museums, all of which may be obtained by Mosaic. The Louvre – although not the actual museum – was voted the best World Wide Web site in 1994 and, gradually, more of the world's leading museums are creating Internet databases containing high quality photographs of their collections. The UK Crafts Council is making available on the Internet its catalogue of 35,000 slides.

The Internet offers a new outlet for artistic skills; some of the most popular servers are those which are attractively designed and take advantage of the technology. Many contemporary artists see the Internet as a gallery for their work: for instance an AIDS charity invites artists to contribute digital works to its Internet gallery. The concept of the Net as a gallery will probably grow. Students with art and design skills will be in demand to design electronic pages. Students could soon be submitting their work to on-line exhibitions, participating in international group work and using the Net as a critical forum.

These ideas are being explored at De Montfort University Leicester, a partner in Project Connect. Students' sketchbooks of visual evidence could be electronic and include work accessed via networks. More and more galleries will be providing tasters of their exhibits on-line, and allowing schools cheaply to download images and text, with the chance to buy CD-ROMs of collections or to order a customised collection for on-line delivery.

Images will be available from all over the world on the Internet and requests for particular images can be posted on art newsgroup areas, with replies often received the same day. Lesson plans for art education (and other curriculum areas) will be available. Coursework could be sent to moderators for assessment, avoiding time-consuming visits to schools.

MUSIC

Communications technologies offer enrichment opportunities for two main areas of the music curriculum: performing and composing; listening and appraising. As they work, students will be learning to control sounds, to compose, refine, record and communicate, to develop knowledge of music from different times and places, and to respond to and evaluate music.

The Internet's many music archives include jazz, classical, world music, and American folk/blues material. A recent development has been the creation of Web servers for rock bands such as the Rolling Stones and Nirvana, with photographs, text and sound clips from albums and live performances. There are many discussion groups devoted to a range of music – from classical European to Indian.

Data transfer times and current compression levels make acquiring music files time-consuming and relatively expensive, but within two years improvements in communications technologies may make the Internet a more convenient way to buy music and to publish and exchange MIDI files. The prospect of making compositions and performances available at low cost to millions of people will then be irresistible to thousands of performers who have failed to achieve recognition through established record companies. The prospect naturally alarms the music industry.

There will be a vast 'soup' of sounds owned by no one, to be sampled, synthesised and experimented with. Such will be the range of interests catered for on the Internet that students will be able to join discussion groups and obtain information about any type of music and any individual band. Students will be exchanging sound files of compositions and taking part in on-line concerts. Will we see an Internet Performing Arts School?

PHYSICAL EDUCATION

Sport is discussed at length on the Internet. The quality of the debate varies from the trivial fan worship to serious discussions of diet and training methods.

The national curriculum requires students to take part in games, gymnastics, dance, swimming, athletics, outdoor and adventure activities. There are UK football team Internet servers and conferences on a range of sports for students to share knowledge, experience and opinions and debate the finer points of football and tennis. Communications technologies can be used in discussing healthy lifestyles, in planning, undertaking and monitoring a safe, health-related exercise programme, in planning a journey, creating challenges for others and evaluating aspects of dance.

The potential exists for collaborative PE-based project work on gathering, exchanging and analysing data on personal fitness, pulse rates and times/distances in athletics. It will be increasingly easy to add to and download skill training videos from sports archives. Access to advice on sports medicine will be available across the network.

INFORMATION SKILLS

Whether 'caught or taught', skills to navigate through, select, assess, manipulate and evaluate information will develop as learners use communications technologies. These skills will form the basis of national economic survival in the information- and knowledge-based economy of the 21st century. Access to an information source such as the Internet can be a motivator for students and encourage independence and autonomy. The national curriculum encourages teachers to develop autonomous users of IT. Open learning, flexible learning and individualised learning are empty phrases if students are not given a coherent and comprehensive grounding in information skills. To introduce something like the Internet or CD-ROM without preparation of both staff and students is the equivalent of giving them a car but not teaching them how to drive.

Information skills have to be taught throughout the institution year after year and developed within all subjects. The delivery of the skills is not just the province of the librarian but that of all teachers. The skills have to be introduced, explained and practised, then continued in greater depth at a basic level year by year and curriculum area by curriculum area. An effective whole-school/college policy on information skills improves students' ability to seek, process and use information, and enhances their learning in other areas. Learning to learn is a powerful aid to improving proficiency across the entire curriculum.

Students and staff need to know:
- how best to frame a question
- which sources to use
- which sources to reject
- how to formulate a search
- how to discover answers to questions
- how to read appropriately and purposefully
- how to store information
- how to combine information with previously acquired material
- the difference between originality and plagiarism
- how to incorporate new material into a current assignment
- how to make appropriate notes
- how to use a variety of styles for their final presentation.

CONNECTING TO THE INTERNET

INTERNET SERVICE PROVIDERS

Different types of access to the Internet are provided for a variety of users – from individuals to large organisations. Each service provider charges different rates for connecting in various ways, such as a dialled connection using a modem and a standard telephone line, a dedicated leased line and ISDN (Integrated Services Digital Network). BBS-style access (sometimes e-mail only) is usually time-charged but an Internet service provider (ISP) usually offers a fixed-rate service. Internet connection and subscription charges may also depend on how much the service is used per day, what type of ser-vices are used (eg e-mail only) and how you connect to the Internet. They also vary almost from week to week owing to the competition between service providers; advice is available from service providers, in the specialist press, from IT centres or NCET.

HOW AN INTERNET SERVICE PROVIDER WORKS

The ISP provides a dial-up telephone number, called a point of presence (PoP). The user runs software to establish a dial-up tele-phone link called a SLIP or PPP connection, and the ISP takes care of

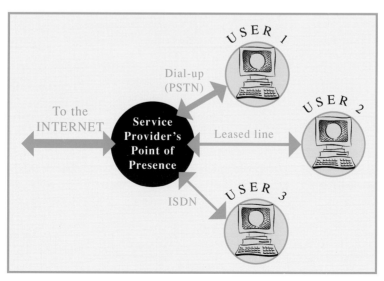

routing the messages into the Internet. Large ISPs provides several PoPs scattered across the country to allow more users local call access. All the routing, forwarding and other information is handled by the Internet service provider and is invisible to the user. All you have to think about is which services you want to receive and what software you will need to have in order to use those services.

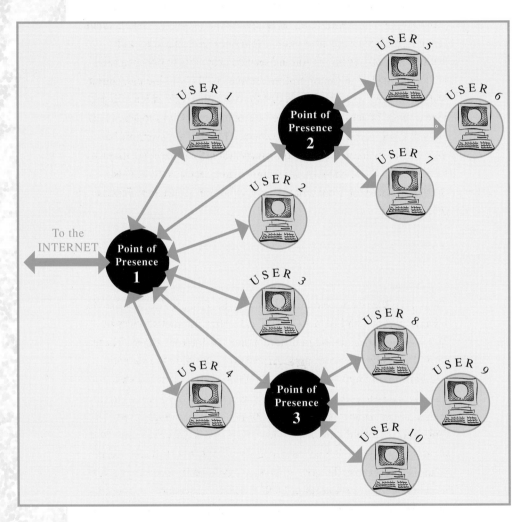

Most Internet service providers offer:
- an e-mail store and forward system, so that your mail is kept until you call the ISP
- a Usenet news feed which, when you call the system, allows you to select messages from special interest newsgroups
- full access to the Internet using standard applications such as Telnet and FTP.

Not all providers will give you direct access to the Internet. Some will route you through a gateway. This means that anything you download will go to the computer run by your provider and then you will have to download it to your machine from there.

Some on-line service providers, such as CIX and CompuServe, have their own 'closed' conferences and information services. Some also provide access to the Internet, although this may be limited to a small range of services, such as e-mail, Usenet newsgroup access and Telnet, but competition is forcing service providers to enhance services provided. The use of on-line services is likely to increase significantly in 1995 with the advent of Microsoft Network which will provide a range of services including Internet access. Links to Microsoft Network will be built into Windows 95. This might reasonably be expected to overcome the inertia which currently hinders the majority of PC users with modems from using on-line services. It will also provide a stable environment for on-line business activities. Further details are on

```
http://www.microsoft.com/pages/services/msnet/
                    msnintro.htm
```

There are three main commercial Internet service providers in the UK – Demon, Pipex and EUnet GB (BT is to offer Internet services in 1995) – each specialising in different areas of Internet access. These providers make their own arrangements for obtaining transatlantic bandwidths and high-speed links. They also make them available to other service suppliers such as CityScape, BBC, Easynet, who in turn provide Internet access. For other Internet service providers see Appendix A. JANET (Joint Academic NETwork Services) also offers an affiliated connection scheme to colleges of further education and schools. In this case the host university would be licensed to provide a college with a connection to JANET via the university, and hence to the Internet. The school or college would have to come to an arrangement with the host – contact UKERNA for advice.

UK Internet providers are co-operating to provide a single neutral interconnection point between service providers instead of the existing web of links. This is expected to increase the efficiency of the connection. BT Internet Services, Demon, EUnet, Pipex and

UKERNA (the organisation behind JANET) are the founder members of this initiative known as 'Linx'.

DEMON

Demon was set up to enable individual home users to connect to the Internet; the company specialises in small, low-volume dialled services. Demon has 13 PoPs, including London, Birmingham, Warrington (within the local call area for Manchester and Liverpool) and Edinburgh and an ambitious plan for 600 'virtual' points of presence, making most users within local call access.

PIPEX

Pipex specialises in corporate connections to the Internet using leased lines, routing software and ISDN; the company also provides some colleges and universities around the UK with access to the Internet. Pipex has six points of presence: Cambridge, Birmingham, West London, East London and Edinburgh and Warrington.

EUNET

EUnet is part of the largest Internet provider in Europe, and supports many of the connections between the UK, Europe and the rest of the world. The company specialises in connecting large organisational networks to the Internet. EUnet currently has points of presence all over the UK and some elsewhere in Europe.

TYPES OF CONNECTION

There are many different ways to connect to an Internet service provider, some of which have already been mentioned. Which one you choose depends entirely on what you want to use the Internet for, and how much use you expect to make of it. These factors will have a direct relation to the cost of the connection you need to make.

STANDARD DIAL-UP CONNECTION

The basic connection method is to dial an Internet service provider using a stand-alone computer and a fast modem (at least 14,400 baud) over a standard telephone line. This is cheap and easy – ideal if you only use the Internet occasionally from home or at school for awareness-raising. With the appropriate software, you can connect almost any type of computer to the Internet in this way. This method is normally used to set up one computer to handle the whole Internet connection, including sending and receiving e-mail, but of course the larger the school or college, the more access is restricted and telephone costs are unpredictable. NCET's information sheet *Choosing and Using Modems* provides guidance on buying a modem.

E-MAIL AND USENET NEWS ONLY

This type of access is normally the same as a standard dial-up connection without the facility to use remote log-in services such as Telnet, FTP and World Wide Web. Companies such as PMS Dialnet and Research Machines include Internet mail in their products, so many schools and colleges already have Internet mail access built into systems used by the examinations officer, secretary or IT manager. The systems often include off-line readers enabling messages to be collected and stored while connected, then read at leisure with the computer off-line. E-mail forwarding is an extension of the standard dial-up service, allowing you to register a 'world-wide domain name' (such as yourco.com) and to have all your e-mail forwarded to your computer, and then perhaps around your internal network. It does not give computers on your network access to the Internet, just to e-mail.

RESERVED LINE

A reserved line connection provides an extra level of security beyond a standard dialled connection, since it guarantees that you will be able to connect to the Internet on demand. A normal dialled connection has to wait for a free line at the PoP you are dialling. You can also ask the Internet service provider to call you on a reserved line when the PoP receives incoming e-mail or remote connection such as Telnet or Gopher.

LEASED LINE

A leased line provides you with a permanent connection to the Internet service provider and hence to the Internet. This gives instant access to the Internet from your computer or (more usually) from your network of computers. E-mail and Usenet news is transferred as it arrives, and incoming or outgoing Internet connections can be made without having to set up and initiate the connection. A leased line is usually faster – often as much as four times faster – than a standard dialled connection; it is ideally suited to heavy and distributed use and enables costs to be budgeted. A leased line costs from £4,000 per year.

ISDN (INTEGRATED SERVICES DIGITAL NETWORK)

ISDN is ideal for high volume use where a permanent connection to the Internet is not wanted. It is a solution favoured by some schools connecting to JANET via universities. The connection set-up time is less than a second, allowing 'virtual networks' where connections are made automatically on demand. ISDN access to the Net may increase as terminal adaptor standards become widespread and this will help to make multimedia access more practicable for schools, and will pro-vide a cost-effective alternative to a leased line. Basic ISDN at 64kb/second is only marginally faster than using a 28,800 modem with compression, but additional bandwidth can easily be added by renting additional ISDN lines. ISDN from BT costs £300 installation, £84 per quarter plus approximately double the telephone on-line charges (February 1995 prices). Schools and colleges may be installing ISDN lines for other uses, eg video surveillance or digital telephones.

ADVANTAGES AND DISADVANTAGES OF THE DIFFERENT TYPES OF CONNECTION

It is important to consider how much use you expect to get out of the Internet, and to choose your connection method accordingly.

Electronic mail and Usenet news are the two most popular types of data transferred. Both types can be stored and sent in batches to your computer when you connect to the service provider. This means you can periodically call a PoP to collect your e-mail and Usenet news, and log off (disconnect) as soon as the information has been trans-ferred, so keeping your telephone charges to a minimum.

Applications such as WWW, Telnet, FTP and Gopher require you to log in to a remote computer, so you must have a connection to the Internet all the time you are using them. The information cannot nor-mally be batched in any way unless you can pre-define your needs so that an independent server can handle your request automatically and then send the results to your computer later.

The table below gives a rough guide to each method of connection and the types of information for which each is best suited.

Connection type	Advantages	Disadvantages	Suggested use
Dial up On demand	Inexpensive Easy to set up and use Ideal for occasional, home and individual use	Slow data transfer Slow connection to the Internet Stand-alone connection only to Internet	Light e-mail Light Usenet news feed Occasional Telnet/FTP/Gopher/WWW access
Reserved line On demand	As above Ideal for occasional use where guaranteed access is needed	As above	Light e-mail Light Usenet news feed Light/ medium Telnet/FTP/Gopher/WWW access
Mail forwarding On demand	Inexpensive, convenient e-mail access for a group of users and computers Ideal for occasional use where guaranteed access is needed	As above	Medium e-mail for multiple users No/light Usenet news feed Occasional Telnet/FTP/Gopher/WWW access
Leased line Permanent	Fast data transfer Enables networks to be connected Permanent, fuss-free unlimited access Costs predictable	Expensive	Heavy e-mail Heavy Usenet news feed Heavy Telnet/FTP/Gopher/WWW access
ISDN On demand	Fast data transfer Ideal for high volume users who do not need permanent access Quick connection Lines can be doubled to increase bandwidth	Expensive	Heavy e-mail Heavy Usenet news feed Regular Telnet/FTP/Gopher/WWW access

INTERNET ACCESS SOFTWARE

Software and interfaces for accessing the Internet now exist for most major computer types, including IBM-compatible PC (DOS or Windows), Apple Macintosh and Commodore Amiga. The software you need will depend on how you access the Internet.

If you are connecting a single computer to the Internet using a dial-up line, you will need special software to send and receive Internet data over standard telephone lines. The software provides the interface to the Internet. This method of access is supported by all types of computer. E-mail and Usenet news are automatically transferred when you dial up, and you can read them off-line (ie when you are not on the phone).

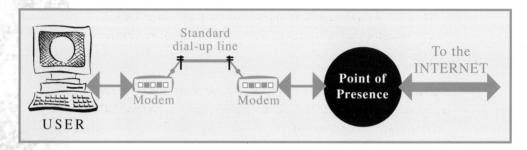

If you are connecting via a leased line, your computer is probably on a network. The network will be connected to a router, a small box which transfers Internet data packets between your internal network and the leased line to the service provider's PoP. Normally only networks are connected to an ISP by leased line.

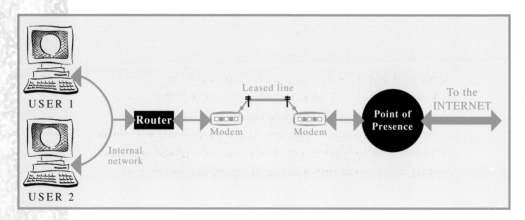

IBM PC – DOS-BASED CONNECTION

A DOS-based connection to the Internet usually gives you a minimal interface, providing only e-mail and Usenet news transfer, plus FTP and Telnet connections. You cannot normally use a package such as Gopher or Mosaic when using a DOS-based interface (but see Lynx, page 43). Using FTP in a multi-tasking manner, however, it is possible to send and receive e-mail and Usenet news at the same time as retrieving files.

IBM PC – WINDOWS-BASED CONNECTION

A Windows-based connection comes in two parts.
- The first part is a WinSock module (Windows socket) which supports the routing of Internet data packets via the telephone line, like a router on a leased line.
- The second part is a suite of application programs for using and accessing Internet services such as e-mail, Usenet news, Gopher, WWW and FTP.

You can use all the application programs within a network on a leased line connection and, since they all run under Windows, you will have a multi-tasking Internet connection.

ACORN

Users of Acorn machines can expect not only full Internet access but also facilities which users appreciate such as universal rendering, which detects the type of file selected and transparently opens an appropriate application. Contact Acorn (01223 254254) for latest details.

APPLE MACINTOSH

Apple's eWorld is a subscription service for standalone computers and modems up to 9600 baud and includes e-mail, Usenet news, Gopher, Mosaic and FTP. Other Apple software provides access to the Internet via a dialled connection which is completely transparent to the user. The software automatically dials the PoP and initiates the connection when you first open one of the application programs.

FINDING INFORMATION ON THE INTERNET

4

'The information just flies at you.'

Teacher at Brooke Weston College, Corby

The Internet allows large quantities of information to be transferred between computers all over the world. It has been estimated that a four-and-a-half-mile line of lorries would have been needed to carry the equivalent of 22 million thick paperbacks of information that moved on the US Internet computer network in one month (*Guardian,* 30 July 1994). Its sheer size – there are already over a million sites in about 150 countries – means that it holds huge quantities of information on all kinds of topics. Getting information out of it has been compared to trying to get a glass of water out of a fire hose. Fortunately there are various tools to select and pour the information into your glass.

DATA TYPES

Data on the Internet can be categorised as unformatted text (or numerical data), formatted text (which comes in a variety of file formats and is more difficult to transfer), graphics (photographs, images, charts and graphs – usually transferred in standard JPEG or GIF format), audio (music and voice, radio, even concerts) or video (transferred in standard MPEG format). Graphics and audio take much longer to transfer than text, and video considerably longer than other forms of data, so the time and costs involved may outweigh the quality of the information you receive.

The actual speed of transfer depends on the transfer means (and sometimes on the congestion of the route). The table below shows estimated times to transfer the uncompressed contents of a CD-ROM, ie 250,000 A4 pages of text, one hour of hi-fi audio or 45 minutes of video. It also demonstrates the speed of current communications technologies, (typically a 14,400 modem), compared to older models, but also the data transfer speeds required for video on demand – the core element of an information superhighway to the home. Nynex, for example, is installing 600 Mb/s fibre optic routes around Manchester, fast enough in theory for the contents of a CD-ROM to be transferred in ten seconds.

Transfer means	Transfer rate (bits per second)	Time taken to transfer 650 megabytes
1200 baud modem	1,200	53 days
14400 baud modem	14,400	4 days
single ISDN channel	64,000	24 hours
ISDN2	128,000	12 hours
ISDN30	1,920,000	47 minutes
2Mb/s JANET and ethernet	2,097,152	43 minutes
34 Mb/s ATM	35,651,584	3 minutes
140 Mb/s SuperJANET	142,606,336	45 seconds

MOVING INFORMATION ON THE NET

CLIENT – SERVERS

Most information on the Internet is transferred using the client–server model: the server part of the application runs on a remote computer which has the resources you want; the client part runs on your computer and obtains resources through its other half – the server. The server – whether a large Unix machine in a university or a stand-alone computer in your front room – looks after its library of files and automatically handles requests from other computers. The client helps you to frame a request to the server, manages the communication between the two parts and presents the results to you. But remember that the server is an automaton, and if there is a choice of client software, the one you use may make the difference between a truly frustrating experience and an easy-to-use, valuable service.

FTP (FILE TRANSFER PROTOCOL)

An FTP server, named after the File Transfer Protocol it uses, provides an archive of files (documents or programs) retrievable on request by filename – provided you know the FTP site (the Internet address of the FTP server) and the name of the file you want. This is one of the basic distribution methods on the Internet. Some FTP sites specialise in particular types of file; some mirror other sites (ie replicate their information and structure) to reduce the pressure on popular servers; some act as a national archive to reduce the amount of international network traffic.

FINDING THE RIGHT INFORMATION

Search tools are the 'brain' of the Net: having all that information is pointless if it cannot be located.

ARCHIE

An Archie server provides a searchable filename index to FTP sites, which makes things easier provided you know the name of the file you require or can make a rough guess at the name from the contents. The server needs to be told how to behave during a search, especially to limit the quantity of output. For example, if the file you want exists on a hundred different FTP servers, you do not really need to know about more than half a dozen of them. Telnet will work in this situation, but an Archie client makes it easier. Once Archie has done its name search through an index, you still have to retrieve a copy of your file – probably by FTP – to your chosen site.

GOPHER

Gopher (as in 'Go-fer this, Go-fer that') is a menu-based interface like a filing cabinet. It was developed as a way of providing information to students on a university campus, and most universities now use it as their campus-wide information system. It has a tree structure and works with folders which hold collections of files and other folders. Files can be of any type, although only text files are displayed by the Gopher client. Here is a sample Gopher client – a text-based system running at the University of Warwick:

```
┌─────────────────────────────────────────────────────────┐
│  nte s. Gopie  In ori..iui C i=  2 ).1  │
│                                                         │
│          Root gopher server: gopher.csv.warwick.ac.uk  │
│                                                         │
│ -> 1.  About WINFO (Warwick INFOrmation Service)/       │
│    2.  Search all WINFO entries at Warwick <?>          │
│    3.  Beyond Warwick/                                   │
│    4.  Information About the University of Warwick/      │
│    5.  Information Services at Warwick/                  │
│    6.  Leisure and Retail Services/                      │
│    7.  Miscellaneous/                                    │
│    8.  News & Events/                                    │
│    9.  Telephone, Email & other Directories/            │
│   10.  Welfare Services/                                 │
│                                                         │
└─────────────────────────────────────────────────────────┘
```

On your computer you see a menu, the most basic form of information retrieval interface. Menu items can include files, lists of more files and folders or jump points to other Gopher servers. The figure above shows Apple Macintosh software, but there are clients for PCs as well (for instance, Hgopher, PC Gopher).

Gophers allow the use of 'bookmarks' enabling you to mark files and create your own list of favourite files. You can then go straight to the bookmark and to the file, without wasting time searching again. You can save multiple bookmark files so that you can record 'sets' of pages of useful information.

You can select each of the items shown above to obtain more information about it; for example, clicking on 'Information about the University of Warwick' displays the next list, as illustrated on the top of the page opposite.

Some Gopher servers provide the facility to search file names within the Gopher service they provide, giving quick and easy access to documents. You can search for any word or phrase in the document file name – for example, 'education'. The following folders, all with 'education' in the title, were found.

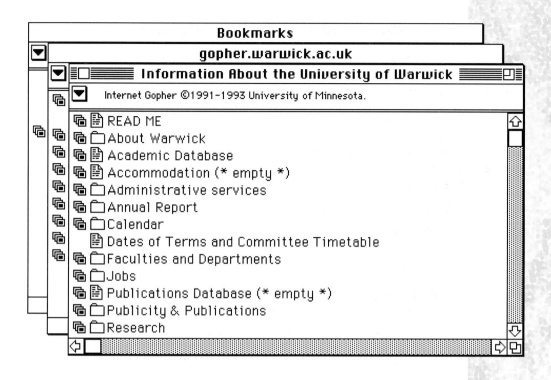

Bookmarks

gopher.warwick.ac.uk

Information About the University of Warwick

Internet Gopher ©1991–1993 University of Minnesota.

- READ ME
- About Warwick
- Academic Database
- Accommodation (* empty *)
- Administrative services
- Annual Report
- Calendar
  - Dates of Terms and Committee Timetable
- Faculties and Departments
- Jobs
- Publications Database (* empty *)
- Publicity & Publications
- Research

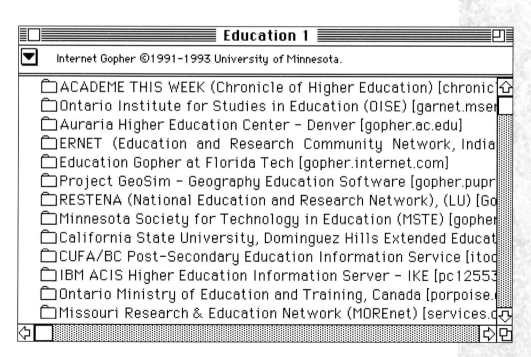

Education 1

Internet Gopher ©1991–1993 University of Minnesota.

- ACADEME THIS WEEK (Chronicle of Higher Education) [chronic
- Ontario Institute for Studies in Education (OISE) [garnet.mser
- Auraria Higher Education Center – Denver [gopher.ac.edu]
- ERNET (Education and Research Community Network, India
- Education Gopher at Florida Tech [gopher.internet.com]
- Project GeoSim – Geography Education Software [gopher.pupr
- RESTENA (National Education and Research Network), (LU) [Go
- Minnesota Society for Technology in Education (MSTE) [gopher
- California State University, Dominguez Hills Extended Educat
- CUFA/BC Post-Secondary Education Information Service [itod
- IBM ACIS Higher Education Information Server – IKE [pc12553
- Ontario Ministry of Education and Training, Canada [porpoise.
- Missouri Research & Education Network (MOREnet) [services.c

WAIS (WIDE AREA INFORMATION SERVER)

WAIS client–server software was developed by Thinking Machines Corporation in California to 'bring the library to the end user's desk' (Brewster Kahle, 1990). A WAIS server indexes the text data it holds on words included in the document, though the document may be text, still or moving images, or sound. WAIS client software enables you to search the index using natural language search terms across user-specified servers anywhere on the Internet; it then reports back with a list of items that match the query in order of relevance, starting from the closest match to your query. You may then select an item and display it or, if you prefer, you may either continue searching, by refining the search, or start a new search.

The drawback of WAIS is that searching large databases on the Internet requires a lot of processing power, so WAIS searching can be very slow. Take care when typing in words for the search, as all words in documents are indexed – even words such as 'and' – which can give misleading relevance feedback when searching. However, the software is still evolving and problems like these are being tackled.

WORLD WIDE WEB

The World Wide Web expands on the Gopher idea of selecting information to view but provides a more friendly, document-based, hypertext-linked interface. The Web is the fastest-growing area of the Internet, with a 700% growth between January and October 1994; it represents 10% of all Internet traffic.

Instead of seeing on your screen a list of available files and folders, you are presented with a page of a document which has hotlinks to other documents and other services embedded in it. A sample screen, taken from the BBC's Networking Club Server, is shown opposite.

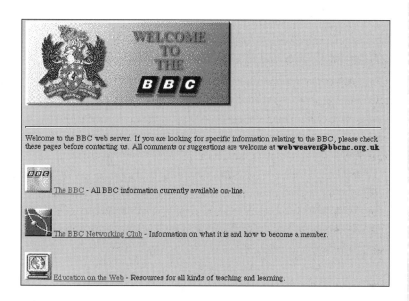

Welcome to the BBC web server. If you are looking for specific information relating to the BBC, please check these pages before contacting us. All comments or suggestions are welcome at **webweaver@bbcnc.org.uk**

The BBC - All BBC information currently available on-line.

The BBC Networking Club - Information on what it is and how to become a member.

Education on the Web - Resources for all kinds of teaching and learning.

UNIFORM RESOURCE LOCATORS

The Web led to the development of URLs (Uniform Resource Locators), which act like telephone numbers. You type in one of 2.1 million – in early 1995 – URLs and the system connects you to that server. For example, the NCET Web server's URL is:

```
http://ncet.csv.warwick.ac.uk/
```

URLs can be included in WWW documents, visible as coloured underlined text or images. Clicking on these 'hotspots' calls up auto-matically the URL and your computer is connected to the document with that unique identifying URL. So, instead of using the bookmark principle, which only references a directory of the information, you can now reference and select the document itself.

BROWSERS

Many consider browsers not only to be the forerunner of the kind of software that will dominate the Internet, but also to be the so-called 'killer' application which will really make the Internet attractive to the general public. The development of easy-to-use browsers has led to the great increase in W3 servers – on average 12 every day.

Using the WWW systems already developed, NCSA Mosaic and commercial versions like Air Mosaic combine in a common interface

many of the existing protocols and interfaces. Mosaic also extends the hypertext linking of the WWW service, incorporating text formatting commands (so that you can have different font sizes and bold, under-line, and italic styles), and also enables you to incorporate graphics into your documents. Here is a sample document – NCET's Home Page:

◄ **NCET** **National Council for Educational Technology**

Welcome to NCET's Information Service

This is a World Wide Web (WWW) based service for accessing educational information technology data, directly over the Net.

To access the latest information from NCET, click here

To access to all other NCET information on the Internet, click here

If you have any comments on this service, or would like further information, please mail Frances_Gullick@ncet.org.uk
To mail any named contact directly at NCET, use their firstname_lastname@ncet.org.uk

---

National Council for Educational Technology
Milburn Hill Road, Science Park, Coventry, CV4 7JJ, England Tel: +44 203 416994, Fax: +44 203 411418

Mosaic incorporates all the features of WWW, including the hyper-text links, plus the text formatting features shown above and the ability to transfer and use (with the appropriate tools, eg Sound Machine for audio files) both sound and video files. With Mosaic, you may also search other information services; Mosaic can interro-gate Gopher and WAIS servers, read and post Usenet messages, and even send and receive mail – all through the Internet and using the same common interface. The hotlist in Mosaic (a list of stored URLs to specified pages, giving you quick access to the documents you add to the hotlist) is similar to the Gopher bookmark system.

Netscape is an improved version of Mosaic. The software is more robust, easier-to-use and faster than Mosaic; you can also begin to read documents before the file transfer is complete. Current versions are free but later versions will be sold commercially; however, the developers of Netscape have stated that there will always be a free version of it for educational users.

Lynx is a hypertext browser program that permits non-graphical access to information on the WWW servers. Because it is text-based, it is often referred to as a 'line browser'. Line browsers are faster than graphical browsers like Mosaic. It is useful if you do not have a full connection to the Internet and are using Telnet to connect to a remote host. Your computer provides a screen and keyboard for the remote computer. You move around the hypertext links using the arrow keys. Some hosts highlight the hypertext links, so you can select a link and press the <ENTER> key. Others will number the links, and enclose them in square brackets, for example 'Educational sources' [1]. Just enter the number of each link to go to that resource.

SEARCH ENGINES

Lycos is very precise and enables fast searches (seconds rather than minutes) to take place across the 2.1 million unique URLs it has located on the WWW. You can search titles and content simply by typing in a word, eg volcanoes, Spain, fascism. Lycos will also make some decisions, about which finds to list for you based on frequency of the search words. Lycos uses a piece of exploratory software called a web crawler to move across the Net indexing, discovering, notating and reporting. The Lycos URL is:

```
http://lycos.cs.cmu.edu/
```

It is one of the most useful URLs and has been nominated for the Best of the Web 1995 Awards. Consequently the Lycos server is a busy site, particularly during the US day, and you may not always be allowed access to it. Lycos is excellent for demonstrating the sheer amount of information on the Net: ask people to name a subject that interests them and show how much there is about it.

Knowbots (knowledge robots) are intelligent agents and they have been brought into being for a very good reason. The main problem with something of the range and scope of the Internet is that most of the material is of no immediate interest. The knowbot's task is to take your instructions, travel round the network looking for material that will interest you and then report back on what it has found. Because so much of the material is new and changing, the knowbot is working most of the time. Undoubtedly such search tools, which save time and increase precision, will be important aids to Internet use and will be refined.

ON-LINE FORMS

With both Mosaic and Netscape you can send information back to the server using on-line forms. Commercial users have not been slow in spotting the marketing opportunities of this while the World Data Centre for Marine Geology and Geophysics has implemented this on their server at:

```
http:// www.ngdc.noaa.gov/mgg/geo/sys.html
```

They offer the 'Meta-Index search engine' for a full text keyword search to retrieve data from their catalogue as well as an option to design your own form with fields selected from a list of terms. You point and click to select the fields. There is a default form available as well for simple queries. Boolean operators (such as 'and', 'or') can be incorporated into the search.

TOWARDS AN EVALUATION

5

There is no quantitative evidence of the impact and benefits of the Internet on UK education to date. Indeed, some people are sceptical, arguing that the Internet is too disorganised, the information on it inaccurate and incomplete, and time spent looking for information or even e-mailing better spent in other ways. However, from NCET's work with pilot projects in the UK and observing Internet usage world-wide for education, some tentative preliminary lessons can be learnt which provide pointers to the successful exploitation of the Internet. More research and evaluation is needed as educational use of the Internet grows.

HOW THE INTERNET WORKS FOR EDUCATION

- The Internet adds value to learning when there is a need for topical, changing or obscure information and for rapid access to resources not available locally. Information is obtainable both from remote databases and from e-mailing and conferencing and, in some cases, can cost less than it would via print, CD-ROM and television.

- Projects involving Internet use can motivate, develop communication and interpersonal skills and foster mutual under-standing across countries and cultures. Such work does, however, need to be well managed, focused and time-limited and to exploit the Internet's unique features.

- Evidence is emerging that the Internet enables institutions to offer a broader curriculum. It can enable less viable subjects such as law or a third foreign language to be taught by grouping students from different institutions and sharing staff.

- The Internet offers challenges for gifted students and makes it easier for them to meet and discuss issues with intellectual peers around the world, through taking part in conferences and user groups. Many of the remote databases are set up with research students in mind and offer new chances to tackle problems.

- The Internet can help to equip students (and their teachers) to live in a world where the ability to handle information will be an important skill. It also helps them to develop lifelong independent learning skills which they can apply outside formal learning situations.

- The Internet enables isolated teachers to communicate with each other and with support agencies. There is the potential for teachers to exchange lesson plans and ideas which work and for agencies to build up banks of such plans and ideas supported by on-line training.

- Those most penalised by isolation benefit most from access to the Internet. The isolation may be due to disability, living in a rural community, economic and social deprivation. It can change the life of a housebound student or a gifted mathematics student in a rural area. Some exciting projects in Belfast and Bristol involve Internet access for inner-city residents.

- There is more time for Internet-related activities at home than at school or college. About 15% of UK homes have computers. In France, where 26m people have access to the Télétel service in their homes, students make extensive use of homework help-lines, resources and information services. However, home access raises issues of equality of access. Should not every learner be entitled to access to this world and to develop the skills to exploit it?

- Students' age obviously affects how they use the Internet. At primary age, children tend to use Internet e-mail to exchange information for structured projects while older students also use it for independent access to information.

- Introducing the Internet, as with other innovations, involves questions of management, training and deployment of equipment, as has been shown, for example, in CD-ROM in schools schemes. Change takes place when senior management actively support it and when staff are involved in the decision-making. If the Internet is going to make a contribution in schools and colleges it will have to be there with the whole-hearted consent of the staff. Whether access is via stand-alone or networked computers, and who is the 'gatekeeper' are crucial to students' taking to the Internet.

- Small-scale pilot projects in the UK have shown that more time than you might think should be allocated to installation of equipment, overcoming technical problems, making connections to the Internet and staff training.

THE AMERICAN K–12 INITIATIVE

There is emerging evidence of the benefits for teaching and learning to be gained from Internet use in American schools and colleges, although to date there are few longitudinal studies. It is in the USA that the use of the Internet is most developed, with an estimated 250,000 teachers and students who are regular Internet users. The uses of the Internet in North America indicate how use of the Internet might develop in Europe and the UK, but there are key differences, notably educational cultures, telecommunications infrastructures and whether or not there is a national curriculum.

K–12 is the American kindergarten to Grade 12 school structure – ages 5 to 18 years. American Congress legislation now extends the Internet to schools, so the high speed communications backbone, NSFNet, can be used to provide educational services to schools. A large number of K–12 projects have been set up to support teachers and students with educational resources including e-mail, bulletin board services, servers and/or pointers to servers with curriculum and relevant reference materials. Individual schools are setting up World Wide Web servers. Many state-sponsored projects offer training schemes and help to teachers to enable them to use the Internet effectively.

The Stanford University Education Server:

```
http://akebono.stanford.edu/yahoo/
education/k-12
```

and Rice University Gopher:

```
gopher://riceinfo.rice.edu/subject
```

provide many K–12 materials and pointers to other curriculum resources. An interesting area to watch is GENII (accessible from the above Stanford University Menu). GENII (Group Exploring the National Information Infrastructure) aims to provide resources and training for teachers in the latest Internet tools so that they can use them effectively in their teaching.

The most notable K–12 projects are state-wide initiatives that work in tandem with universities and research institutions, often providing networked access to the Internet for whole classrooms – for example, TENET in Texas, PEN in Virginia, FIRN in Florida, and the California Technology Project. About 60% of Internet projects in the US are state initiatives. (For a full list of other K–12 activities send an e-mail to ERIC: npreston@suvm.acs.syr.edu.) As well as addressing important issues in resource management, training and teaching method, the projects explore the thorny issues of acceptable user policies, the legal foundation for Internet use and electronic privacy for students. Appendix B includes a selection of references to documents describing the Internet experiences of individual schools.

A more comprehensive study was carried out at Carnegie Mellon University on the use of the Internet in K–12 education. It indicates that, given adequate access to and training on the Internet, teachers have been able to perform activities that would not be possible without the Internet. It has on the whole encouraged successful collaborative working practices and an exchange of viewpoints. Teaching styles often had to change to accommodate the students' need for higher order thinking skills, with teachers acting more as facilitators, to guide the student learning process.

For students, regardless of age, use of the Internet has expanded their horizons, enabling them to explore materials from different perspectives and leading to collaborative working of a higher quality, rather than fostering competition. Students seem more motivated when, for example, they write essays with communication rather than evaluation as a goal.

The American trend to 'restructure' the curriculum in schools has at its heart a pedagogical approach that puts the student at the centre of the learning process. The curriculum is based on student interests, to increase motivation and promote creative problem-solving and analytical thinking skills. The Carnegie Mellon study focused on a school with students who had special education needs and a varied socio-economic background. The findings showed that the teachers felt the Internet could be a useful tool for the restructuring process. Students were enthusiastic in their use of the Internet to expand their knowledge, although delays in delivering and installing equipment and a lack of knowledge of Internet tools were sources of frustration. Another study sponsored by the National Science Foundation suggested that networks and Internet resources form a useful channel for information to support open-ended school work.

In both national systematic studies published on K–12 so far (Carnegie Mellon and Centre for Technology in Education), findings are that robust, networked access to NSFNet works best with a partner university being involved as the gateway to the backbone. In the UK this model could be emulated by schools and local education authorities linking with neighbouring universities using the SuperJANET backbone, as is already happening in Kent, Leicester (Project Connect), Aberystwyth, Liverpool and Hertfordshire.

'The Internet and Schools: A Survey of Networking Activities', a paper given at the Internet Society's INET '94 Conference in Prague by Tracy LaQuey Parker of Cisco Systems, summarises with examples the positive effects of the Internet on US education, not just on the curriculum but also on training, administration and the community. The full text of the paper can be found on the World Wide Web at:

```
http://sunsite.unc.edu/cisco/
        tracy-article.html
```

In it, it is argued that, for the Internet to be integrated successfully into schools, benefits must be shown for all aspects of education:

administrative, professional development, instructional and community involvement. The more solutions Internet access provides, the more it will be integrated. Here are four examples described by Tracy LaQuey Parker.

ADMINISTRATIVE USES

'Since up to 20% of a school's students move annually, there are significant time and financial savings to be made if records are held electronically; the average time spent transferring a record using the current system is 24 days. Using Electronic Document Interexchange for transferring standardised student records across the Internet, the cost drops from the current average $15 per transferred record to $4. With savings like these, a business case can certainly be made for installing a network infrastructure and a link to the Internet.'

PROFESSIONAL DEVELOPMENT

'Pat Gathright, journalism teacher at MacArthur High School in San Antonio, Texas, collaborates with other Internet-connected journalism teachers across Texas and the US.

"I have the sole responsibility on my campus for the yearbook, newspaper, Journalism I, and Photojournalism," she says. "Few of my fellow teachers can come close to understanding what my job is like or help me with some of the problems I face each day. But I know that I can log onto the Internet and share with my journalism friends across the state a desktop publishing trick that I learned at a workshop, a place to find information on a story my students are working on, or just news about my day."

Before the Net existed, journalism teachers like Ms Gathright met once a year at their annual conference in Austin. Now many teachers meet on-line 24 hours a day, 365 days a year.'

BENEFITS FOR STUDENTS

'Rachel Weston, a 7th Grader at Georgetown Day School in Washington DC, wrote in a recent essay how the Internet has changed her life. "As I flipped through my e-mail messages one morning I suddenly received a new one entitled 'The Sydney Bush Fires'. The mail was from my Australian keypal, and he was telling me and some of his other keypals what it was like to be experiencing the bush fires that were burning all round Sydney." Rachel goes on to describe the communication that took place between her friend and herself on Internet Relay Chat, his stories of the fires and how close they got to his house. In addition to the live reports, she clipped relevant newspaper articles. "All week long the information about the Sydney fires that I brought to current events in my social studies class was more up to date than anything in the newspapers," she said.'

COMMUNITY OUTREACH

'Some schools and network projects are encouraging parents to become involved and have offered community access via dial-up accounts to school systems. Homework assignment archives, schedules, calendars, lunch menus, etc, are just some of the things that network projects are encouraging parents to become involved and have offered community access via dial-up accounts to school systems. Homework assignment archives, schedules, calendars, lunch menus, etc, are just some of the things that can be made publicly available. Additionally, teachers are more accessible via electronic mail for parent/teacher conferences. While community access is not as well defined or publicised yet, it is a crucial part of the educational and community building use of the Internet. Several schools are experimenting with providing low-cost accounts (to help pay for their networking costs) to parents and members of the surrounding community to enable access to local school information and the Internet.'

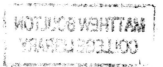

THE INTERNET OF THE FUTURE

'The most dramatic discontinuity will come in the telecommunications arena. The shift from analogue to digital networks will bring with it incredible improvements in communications ubiquity, quality and cost.'

The beginning of a new media industry –
A report from the Hakone Forum, 1992, p 13

'The future of the PC is as a personal communications device.'

Bill Gates, Microsoft, 1994

'The education sector meltdown is being prompted by the availability of communication and information. The education sector will no longer be constrained by distance, time and country, and will evolve to become a truly international activity. As a result it will lose its monopolies.'

Michael Gell and Peter Cochrane, 'Future shocks',
Training Tomorrow, January 1995

It is the convergence of familiar technologies like the television, computer and telephone which makes the Internet possible and challenges us to imagine new ways of thinking, communicating, learning and working. When information is created, stored, sent and received in digital form (ie as a series of zeroes and ones) it becomes easier to store and manipulate. It is too early to predict what this convergence will mean for education, or for entertainment and work. Most predictions about technology have turned out to be wrong: Bell thought he had invented the radio and imagined people listening to concerts gathered around their telephone and Marconi believed his radio would be most useful as a means of ship-to-shore communication. Pioneers tend to concentrate on the technology, underestimating what users might do with it and its social, political, historical and economic context. The Internet is developing all the time and what it might look like in a few years is linked to other technical developments such as portability, multimedia and communications technologies and wider shaping factors such as social, political and commercial concerns. Simon Cook's description of the Internet in Chapter 1 could well bear no resemblance to it in a year's time.

The Internet gives us a glimpse of future possibilities. It offers low-cost access to a wide range of free information and facilities. Despite all the hype, the service is patchy, largely American in content, not guaranteed and it depends largely upon altruism and generosity which conflict with notions of the market and added value. Will commercial and political interests permit this to continue? As broadband communications reach homes, for example, will politicians allow 'camcorder activists' freely to broadcast their materials over the network? Will current Internet philosophies resist commercial pressures on the Internet and its irresistible lure of low-cost access to millions of consumers? The indications are that the answer to both these questions is No.

There is at present no standardised secure billing system to charge users for information and some argue that this inhibits the development of added-value services, more useful information, quality controls over content and investment in the infrastructure to enable it to avoid gridlock. This is partly because of the US government's reluctance to see the powerful encryption methods available to its enemies or potential enemies. The situation is changing fast, and in November 1994 for the first time the majority of new Web servers were commercial and the prediction for the next twelve months is for an explosion of on-line commerce and systems enabling providers to receive payment for products.

As security improves, the Internet may provide lower-cost access to EDI (Electronic Data Interchange). This is likely to be of interest to cost-conscious school and college administrators as well as to researchers who may be using expensive proprietary EDI services. IBM, DEC and others are working on common standards for protocols. In the meantime we already have e-mail software that permits document exchange over the Internet without losing formatting (eg Eudora, Mail It 2, Pegasus). And shareware versions of data encryption software are already available to help with data security (eg PGP, Pretty Good Privacy). In fact, some of this software is so good that it is beginning to worry the American government.

Some people have suggested that the present situation where you can roam the world by Internet virtually free is just an interim period rather like those few years in the American west when the frontiers of the country were being settled. The issues confronting everyone in the information society are important ones. Do we have a right to access? Should access be limited to the 'haves'? Who regulates the networks? Indeed, should there be any regulation at all?

Nevertheless, the British creator of the Web, Tim Berners-Lee, is optimistic about its future:

'I hope the Web will reverse some of the harm that has been done by television. It will enable people to explore, and to be creative, and to find out what information they really want as opposed to being bombarded with information they are appeased by but have no control over. I think it will be a really rich resource.'

'The Whole World in his Hands',
Personal Computer World, December 1994, p 382

More and more individuals, schools, colleges and information and service providers will publish on their own WWW servers, thus building up the critical mass of useful and relevant material, and ultimately making life without access to the Internet inconceivable. Some ISPs like Cityscape offer free WWW home pages to subscribers. Microsoft has recently introduced an add-on for its word-processing package, 'Internet Assistant for Word', enabling users to write HTML pages on the Web without learning to use new software. Free software for creating WWW pages is available over the Internet as well, together with free advice and guidance on design and content. This suggests that output to the Web may be almost as frequent and just as simple as to printers or fax.

It is inevitable that telephone tariffs will be reduced owing to the sheer capacity of optical fibre – 47,000 phone calls can be carried simultaneously over a fibre thinner than a human hair. Europe Union predictions of 10% of the population teleworking are built on this assumption. The capacity means that enormous amounts of information can be transferred at high speed and low cost. This is the logic behind one vision of the information society:

'Information on demand. Any place. Any time. In the right format. At the right price. Plus instant gratification. You hit the key. You say the word. You get a response.'

Peter Cochrane, BT, 1994

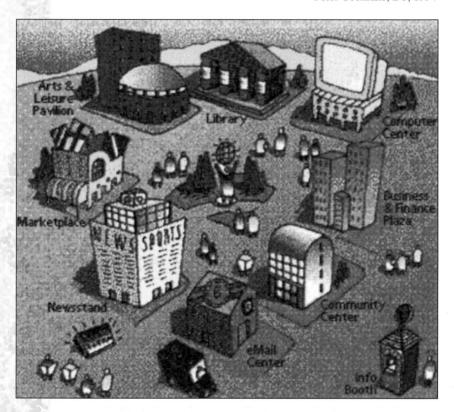

The 'instant gratification' part of the vision will come about when interfaces improve. New graphical representations of the interface between user and the Internet, as seen with Apple's eWorld and its all-American town and Microsoft's cosy sitting-room, present the user with a very friendly and attractive front-end and make searching easier. The front screen is designed to look familiar, so users can intuitively click on the icon that provides the kind of information they are looking for. As the tools become more powerful they quite rightly become more invisible. Tim Berners-Lee and others see the future of the Web as a single user interface metaphor. This will mean that the boundaries between e-mail, Usenet News and WWW will disappear. In the pipeline are speech-based interfaces to the Net. These will use artificial intelligence and natural language recognition. Filters are being developed to reduce information overload.

AND TEACHING AND LEARNING...?

'We are just getting into this and the children are becoming very excited about the possibilities. We have staff who are starting to take an interest and we hope that we can develop work along the lines of using the Internet as a very active and user-friendly reference facility.'

Chris Thatcher, Potters Green School, Coventry

Constructing visions of the future can be difficult if the focus is the technology – technologies change fast and developments are driven by unpredictable forces. However, with a focus on the learner, on what is learned and on how it is learned, we can say a great deal. The question of access must be considered. A vision for the future must have as its goal the realisation of a superhighway for all: all learners must have access to the information they need and they must be able to do with it what they need for the task in hand. And this will require attention to service infrastructures, to user interfaces and to the ways in which learning is organised.

It is the user's exercise of choice that will determine whether the Internet backbone will expand and high capacity networking take off in homes and schools. John Logie Baird could never have guessed that Baywatch would be the most watched programme in the history of television. Consumers will decide whether the Internet develops into another form of mass entertainment or something more worth while:

'When Gutenberg invented the printing press, it helped generate an information explosion since books could be produced more quickly and more cheaply than ever before. This resulted in the flowering of the Renaissance and the rediscovering of ancient Greek, Roman and Arabic texts that led to establishing modern science and accelerated the move away from feudal societies.'

Tom Foremski, 'Overloaded on the Internet',
Financial Times, 8 November 1994

Technically, the Internet is a new wonder of the world. But it would be fatal to allow the technically-minded to dictate how it should be used and its content. A scenario has been painted in which maths teachers are contacted at home over the Internet by individual students stuck on their homework: how do maths teachers and their families view this prospect? Do we really want video on demand or do we actually like being passive couch potatoes? Will teachers want at their fingertips all the educational materials ever produced on paper or on video?

Until users can be sure to get the information they want in the form they want more or less instantly, the information side of the Internet will not be exploited on a large scale by schools and colleges. It may be that the future will bring many different networks and services to the Internet, tailored to different users. For education, this means high-speed affordable access, intuitive interfaces and tools, and, most important, a critical mass of content relevant to educational needs and ways of working. The technicians will take care of the former; the latter has to be created by practitioners who care about teaching and learning:

'In my view, the best way forward is through local innovation. I do not believe that anyone is in a position to predict or shape the future of education. What we need are illustrations with examples of what schools can do with and through new technology.'

David Wood, *The Classroom of 2015*,
National Commission on Education Briefing 20, October 1993

USEFUL CONTACT ADDRESSES

Information about service providers is subject to change. Details given here are for guidance only and were accurate in January 1995. Inclusion does not imply NCET endorsement. Consult NCET's Enquiry Desk, Internet magazines, local IT centres and professional organisations like ACITT (see below) for latest details.

INTERNET SERVICE PROVIDERS

Acorn Computers
Acorn House
Vision Park
Histon
Cambridge CB4 4AE
Tel: 01223 254254
For details of InterTalk, for Internet access using Acorn computers. Web browser in preparation. Service enables administrator to restrict access to sites, groups and individuals, and includes features to keep on-line costs down.

Apple On-line Services
6 Roundwood Avenue
Stockley Park
Uxbridge
Middlesex UB11 1BB
Tel: 0800 585682
The eWorld service provides full, user-friendly Internet access for Apple users at $8.95 per month plus first two hours' use at $2.95 per hour, thereafter $12.90 per hour.

Atlas Internet
19 Devonshire Street
London W1N 1FS
Tel: 0171 312 0400   Fax: 0171 636 9219
Full Internet facilities offered using PPP – dial-up service, dedicated dial-up, ISDN dial-up, dedicated ISDN. Six PoPs. Service costs

examples: dial-up initial charge £25, annual fee £130. ISDN dial-up £100 registration then £275 annual fee.

BBC Networking Club
PO Box 7
London W3 6XJ
Tel: 0181 576 7799
E-mail: `info@bbcnc.org.uk`
Aimed at schools and home users. Features include full Internet access and its own discussion groups. Cost £25 registration, then £12 per month. Good range of points of presence.

BT
Campus 2000 Internet Service
Network House
Brindley Way
Apsley
Hemel Hempstead
Hertfordshire HP3 9RR
Tel: 01345 626253   Fax: 01442 237811
Campus mail: `01:CBT007`
Dial-up and ISDN educational access to the Internet and comprehensive services for information providers planned.

CableNet
Landscape Studios
Crowhurst
East Sussex TN33 9BX
Tel: 01424 830700
E-mail: `cablenet@landscap.demon.co.uk`
Internet service for cable telephone customers offering permanent on-line access for about £500 per year.

CityScape Internet Services
59 Wycliffe Road
Cambridge CB1 3JE
Tel: 01223 566950   Fax: 01223 566951
E-mail: `sales@cityscape.co.uk`
WWW: `http://www.cityscape.co.uk/`
Popular with schools in UK, easy-to-use software and installation, a good helpline – 24 hour support. £50 joining fee then £180 per year.

Six points of presence. Offering free space on Goldsite Europe server (Europe's largest and busiest commercial server).

CIX (Compulink Information eXchange) Ltd
London House
Ancaster
Llanrwst
Gwynedd LL26 0LD
Tel: 01492 641 961 or 0181 390 8446
E-mail: `cixadmin@cix.compulink.co.uk`
Offers limited Internet access but good off-line readers to simplify e-mail and save telephone costs. £25 registration, subscription £6.25 per month, then £3.20 per hour peak or £2.40 off-peak.

CompuServe
1 Redcliffe Street
PO Box 676
Bristol BS99 1YN
Tel: 0117 976 0681
E-mail: `70006.101@compuserve.com`
Established in 1979, Compuserve is an enormous unparalleled text-based resource with over 2 million members – the largest ISP in the world. Fuller Internet access should be available soon. Service primarily aimed at the business user. Complex price structure depending on services required. £26.45 start-up fee plus £6.50 per month. Basic services free, additional charges per hour for extended services with a surcharge for using 14.4k modems. Free trial membership available.

Delphi Internet
The Elephant House
Hawley Crescent
London NW1 8NP
Tel: 0171 715 7080, 0171 757 7150
E-mail: `ukservice@delphi.com`
Menu-based system of Internet access, which can limit choices. No start-up fee. Cost £10 per month, four hours free, then £4 per hour or £20 per month, 20 hours free, then £1.80 per hour. Surcharges for some services. Free trial service available.

Demon Internet Limited
Gateway House
322 Regents Park Road
Finchley
London N3 2QQ
Tel: 0181 371 1234
E-mail: internet@demon.net
URL: http://www.demon.co.uk/
Considered the cheapest for full dial-up access. £12.50 (+ VAT) registration then £10 (+VAT) per month. Now using Energis (National Grid lines) to provide 600 virtual PoPs (thus local call rates in most areas of UK) as well as 13 regional PoPs.

DIALnet/PMS Communications Ltd
Western House
43 Smallbrook Queensway
Birmingham B5 4HQ
Tel: 0121 624 5050
The leading electronic clearing house in education offers a range of integrated messaging services to schools and colleges, including e-mail and links to the Internet, together with the ability to transfer orders and receive invoices from suppliers.

Easynet
New Accounts Department
39 Whitfield Street
London W1P 5RE
Tel: 0171 209 0990
E-mail: admin@easynet.co.uk
Monthly charge £13.98, yearly £139.59 if you are already member of any on-line service; otherwise start-up charge of £25 + VAT.

The Education Exchange (EdEx)
TCNS Ltd
3 Stroud Road
Wimbledon Park
London SW19 8DQ
Tel: 0181 944 8021   Fax: 0181 944 5029
E-mail: tim@tcns.co.uk
WWW: http://www.galviz.co.uk/

A London-based gateway which tailors Internet resources to students, thus saving time and preventing access to undesirable materials. Direct permanent ISDN or cable connection (ie unlimited use) costs £5,950–£14,500 per year plus installation (from £1,100). Dial-up access for individual users £70 per year, for organisations £310.

EUNet GB
Wilson House
John Wilson Business Park
Whitstable
Kent CT5 3QY
Tel: 01227 475497
E-mail: `sales@Britain.EU.net`
£300 initial charge, then £1,800 per year; ISDN service available at £3,000 per year.
Alternative supplier:
John Stewart
ElectricMail Limited
Orwell House
Cowley Road
Cambridge CB4 4WY
Tel: 01223 420193
E-mail: `info@elmail.co.uk`
WWW: `http://www.britain.eu.net`
There are currently eight points of presence including two in Scotland. ISDN access only available through Canterbury PoP.

Genesis Project Ltd
International Trade Centre, Interpoint
20–24 York Street
Belfast
Northern Ireland BT15 1AQ
Tel: 01232 231622
E-mail: `sales@gpl.com`
WWW: `http://www.gpl.net`
Established IT services provider, Genesis have recently become a Pipex feed for Northern Ireland access. £25 then £15 monthly for 28.8k lines; £10 per month for 14.4k modem connection.

Internet Connection
IBM Global Network
PO Box 1
Rockware Avenue
Greenford
Middlesex UB6 0DW
Tel: 0181 813 0077
E-mail: `inquire@uk.ibm.com`
Full Internet connectivity offered at £10 per month to PC users who
have the new OS/2 Warp software (including three hours' access; £3
per additional hour).

Microsoft Limited
Microsoft Place
Winnersh
Wokingham
Berkshire RG11 5TP
Tel: 01734 270001
E-mail: `davegre@microsoft.com`
WWW: `http://www.ms.com`
For the Web-in-a-Box, on-line services, Internet HTML creation tools
and Internet readers.

Pavilion Internet Plc
Aqua House
24 Old Steine
Brighton
East Sussex BN1 1EL
Tel: 01273 607072
E-mail: `info@pavilion.co.uk`
Initial charge £15, then £12 per month; seven PoPs.

Pipex
Unipalm Ltd
216 Cambridge Science Park
Milton Road
Cambridge CB4 4WA
Tel: 01223 250120
E-mail: `sales@pipex.net`
Internet access using ISDN and routers, but also dial-up access: cost
£50 registration, then £180 per year. Six points of presence in UK.

Many of the other UK access providers get their own Internet connectivity via Pipex (BBCNC, IBMPCUG, Exnet, Genesis, Cityscape, Direct Connection).

Research Machines plc
83 Milton Park
Abingdon
Oxford OX14 4SE
Tel: 01235 826000
WWW: http://www.rmplc.co.uk
The Internet for Learning package includes fixed rate contracts to manage on-line costs, the option of filtered information and support materials to exploit the Internet in the classroom. A full Internet service will be offered in 1995 – initially with a single PoP in Abingdon, Oxfordshire. £25 registration, then £120 per year. Free Web pages for educational institutions.

UKERNA
JANET Liaison Desk
Atlas Centre
Chilton
Didcot
Oxfordshire OX11 OQS
Tel: 01235 445517
For information about JANET.

U-Net Limited
Unit G9
Warrington Business Park
Long Lane
Warrington WA2 8TX
Tel: 01925 633144   Fax: 01925 850420
E-mail: hi@u-net.com
WWW: http://www.u-net.com
Service aimed solely at Windows users; may be useful if you have no local PoP since the Warrington PoP offers 28.8k speed of connection as standard. Initially £12, then £12 monthly or £100 for year, plus VAT.

Zynet
Tel: 01392 426160
Various low-cost options onto the Internet for educational users on a mixture of BT and Eurobell telephone lines. PoP in Exeter, initial charge £20 then £18 monthly.

OTHER ORGANISATIONS

ACITT
Brondale Cottage
5 Spring Gardens
Narberth
Dyfed SA67 7BN
Tel: 0181 698 3713
The National Association for Teachers and Co-ordinators of IT, for help and advice for members.

Novell (UK) Limited
Novell House
London Road
Bracknell
Berkshire RG12 2UY
Tel: 01344 724000
For local area networks and Internet connectivity.

For suppliers of modems, ask for NCET's information sheet *Choosing and using modems.*

CONTRIBUTORS TO THIS PUBLICATION

Jack Kenny, `jackenny@cix.compulink.co.uk`
Richard Ross-Langley, `rrl@minfo.demon.co.uk`
Len Warner, `len@easynet.co.uk`
Tracy LaQuey Parker, Manager, Education Market Development, Cisco Systems, `tparker@cisco.com`

A SELECT
BIBLIOGRAPHY

USEFUL BOOKS FOR GENERAL
REFERENCE

Dern, Daniel, *The Internet Guide for New Users*, McGraw-Hill, 1994,
ISBN 0 07 016510 6

Gilster, Paul, *Finding it on the Internet*, John Wiley, 1994,
ISBN 0 471 03857 1

Hahn, Harley and Stout, Rick, *The Internet Complete Reference*,
McGraw-Hill, 1994, ISBN 0 07 881980 6

Hahn, Harley, and Stout, Rick, *The Internet Golden Directory*,
McGraw-Hill, 1994, ISBN 0 07 882082 0

Krohl, Ed, *The Whole Internet: User's Guide & Catalogue*, O'Reilly
& Associates, 1994, ISBN 1 56592 063 5

Levine, John R., and Baroudi, Carol, *Internet for Dummies*, IDG
Books Worldwide, 1993, ISBN 1 56884 024 1

Mailer, Nicholas, and Dickson, Bruce, *UK School Internet Primer*,
Koeksuster Publications, 1994, ISBN 0 9524072 05
    A readable, concise and useful introduction written from the UK
    perspective for schools wishing to use the Internet. More details
    on their home page:
          `http://www.demon.co.uk/koekie/`

Pope, Ivan, *Internet UK*, Prentice Hall, 1994

Schofield, Sue, *The UK Internet Book*, Addison Wesley, 1994

Schofield, Sue, and Farquharson, Neil, *Modem and Communications
Guidebook*, Future Business Books, 1993, ISBN 1 858700 000

Smith, John, *Directory of Internet Service Providers*, British Library, forthcoming 1995

Vincent, Patrick, *Free stuff on the Internet*, Cariolis Group Books, 1995

MAGAZINES AND NEWSPAPERS

Internet World, Mecklermedia Corporation (monthly)
Internet and Comms Today, £2.95, Paragon Publishing (monthly)
Internet, £1.50, EMAP Business Communications (monthly)
.net The Internet magazine, £2.95, Future Publications (monthly)
Guardian On-line, every Thursday, supplement to the *Guardian*

JOURNAL ARTICLES ABOUT SCHOOL EXPERIENCES

Andres, Yvonne Maries, 'Education on–line', *Executive Educator*, Vol. 15 (6), June 1993

> A programme co-ordinator from Jefferson Junior High School describes uses of FrEdMail, one of the earliest co-operative Internet projects aimed at schools in the US. Since then, FrEdMail has supported projects such as the Global Schoolhouse project which used CU-SeeMe video conferencing software on the Internet. It has also given rise to SCHLnet, a sort of selective Usenet for education that filters out unsuitable newsgroups.

Harris, Judi, 'Using Internet know-how to plan how students will know', *The Computing Teacher*, Vol. 20 (8), May 1993, pp 35–40

> Judi Harris attempts to integrate Internet resources effectively into teaching by structuring 'telecomputing' activities into 15 categories, with sample projects for each. She groups these under broad headings such 'Information collections', 'People exchanges', 'Collaborative problem solving'. An excellent introduction to what to do in the classroom across the curriculum once students and teachers have been connected and trained.

Honey, Margaret, and Henriquez, Andres, *Telecommunications and K–12 educators: findings from a national survey*, Centre for Technology in Education, Bank Street College of Education, New York

The report presents a survey of a systematic attempt to investigate telecommunications activity by taking a nationwide sample. A 27-page questionnaire was developed after consultation with teachers, administrators, and computer and media specialists using telecommunications for student learning. The schools in the sample had an average of 66.5 computers, compared to a national average of 27, and had been using computers for an average of 8.4 years. Computers seem to have been placed mainly in computer labs and classrooms, though some were also found in libraries and administration areas. Half of the teachers used computers in their teaching. About half were also connected to LANs, so the sample showed that the schools involved in telecommunications activity had a technology-rich environment. Teachers were self-motivated and mainly self-taught, and had been using the technology for an average of three years. There seems to have been little telecommunications support at school and district level, though support for general computer-based activities was available. Conferences were the most widely used information resource, but peer group support and other on-line users were also important. Teachers reported that they had made use of Internet projects such as FrEdMail and K–12 Net. A major benefit identified is the ability to confer with other colleagues and share professional experiences and resources. Getting instant curriculum feedback, and keeping abreast of pedagogical, subject and technical information are also strong incentives.

Killan, Crawford, 'Why teachers fear the Net', *Internet World*, November/December 1994, pp 86–87

Killan argues that complex hardware and lack of good training is holding teachers back. Teachers have little time to struggle with obsolete hardware and tricky installation procedures. Pedagogical fears are an additional factor: many teachers are used to a rigid framework for their teaching programmes, prescribing texts, exercises and activities for their students. Providing Internet access with all its resources can subvert a tidy curriculum. Killan thinks the situation will change as technology gets easier and more reliable. The changing economy and job market will make a more flexible curriculum inevitable.

Meizal, Janet, 'High school education and the Internet: the Davis Senior High School experience', *The Impact of Technology on Resource Sharing,* Haworth Press, 1992, pp 137–139

A computer science teacher's experiences of resource sharing and introducing Internet resources for students and teachers in a US equivalent of a British secondary school. Initial findings are that students like the participative nature of Internet, and access has been successful with male and female students of all ethnic groups in the school. This technology has had a positive impact across the curriculum, and has been taken up enthusiastically by biology, maths and modern languages teachers, who have found Internet information resources useful in the curriculum. The most popular newsgroups include subjects like space shuttle, international relations, computer languages, music and ethnic issues. Information overload, lack of information-handling skills, and management of resources are the three areas that need to be addressed before the technology can be exploited productively. The project is ongoing, but at the end of the first year of Internet use, a survey shows that 64% of students had two or more teachers (other than computer science teachers) who assigned work needing computer use compared to less than 2% at the beginning of the year. Access to the Internet seems to have been a catalyst for cross-curricular use of IT.

Merali, Zinat, 'K–12 activities and implications for the UK', *Internet World & Document Delivery World International*, Proceedings of the Second Annual Conference, London, May 1994, pp 136–139

A look at how the UK may benefit from the US experience of K–12 initiatives, a discussion of the infrastructure implications and a resumé of the UK scenario with reference to Internet activities in schools.

Stefansodottir, Lara, 'Internet in Icelandic schools', *Internet World & Document Delivery World International*, Proceedings of the Second Annual Conference, London, May 1994, pp 140–143

A description of the Iceland educational network linking 300 schools to the Internet using dial-up connections. The project addressed installation and initial training needs of individual schools by visiting each one. This was backed up by on-line training courses for teachers on how to use Gopher, e-mail etc – and, for secondary schools, how to teach on-line.

Valauskas, Edward J., 'Education on-line: interactive K–12 computing', *On-line*, Vol. 17 (4) July 1993, pp 89–91

A vision on the lines of 'a day in the life of ...' – what a teacher may encounter in a school fully connected to the Internet, with its bonuses and its problems. The author goes on to describe how 'Kidsphere', a list on the Internet designed for educators, has been used imaginatively in schools, both in the UK and elsewhere.

West, Peter, 'The Mother of all networks', *Teacher Magazine*, Vol. 4 (4) January 1993, pp 19–22

An overview of wide-ranging educational Internet applications in a number of US schools and the issues of access and good practice it raises. The article includes examples of innovative use and is studded with viewpoints from programme co-ordinators and teachers.

GLOSSARY OF TERMS

ARPAnet

Advanced Research Projects Agency Network – a system developed
by the American defence industry in the 1960s as the first resilient
large-scale packet switched network. Precursor to the Internet.

Archie

Archie is an indexing tool for ftp archives. Archie servers like
`archie.doc.ic.ac.uk` tell you where to locate a
publicly-available file anywhere on the Net.

ATM

Asychronous Transfer Mode. A high-speed switching technology that
uses short fixed-length packets called cells to convey video, voice and
data. Fixed-length packets make processing simpler, quicker and predictable, which is essential for time-sensitive services such as voice
and data.

Bandwidth

The range of signal frequencies to indicate how much data can pass
along a channel at one time. Broadband networks, the basis of the
'information superhighway', allow video signals to pass at high
speed; narrowband tend to be text-only and are slower.

BBS

Bulletin board system, also known as computer conferencing: a computer equivalent of a public notice board. You can read and write
messages, store and retrieve files and communicate with other users
and other computers.

Bookmark

A method of saving addresses (eg URLs) that you frequently visit;
similar to the 'hotlist' in Mosaic. Turbogopher and NetScape use the
concept of a 'bookmark'.

Browser

A client program used to search and retrieve information. Mosaic and
Cello are browsers which you can 'point' at URLs.

Chat mode

Where a BBS mediates, using Internet relay chat, a live discussion between simultaneous users on a computer. Users type what they want to say at the keyboard and see the conversation develop on the screen. This is an expensive conferencing option because of telephone costs.

Client

In the context of 'client–server' programs, a client is the software on the user's computer which send commands to the server. The server program carries out the activities that the client software specifies and sends the output, eg information or a file, back to the client program. Gopher, WAIS, WWW and ftp all have clients that you run on your computer in order to talk to the servers.

Computer conferencing

A development of electronic mail designed for supporting many-to-many communication. Computer conferencing software includes features specifically designed to help in the organisation, structuring and retrieval of messages. In particular, messages can be organised under different 'topics'. Search commands can rapidly identify messages with particular keywords in their titles or in the body of the text. Special commands are available to the person responsible for a conference (the moderator) to assist in defining the membership of the conference, to keep the discussion on track, and to schedule the opening and closing of discussion topics. In some systems, messages can be linked to each other (for example, as 'comments').

Conference

On a BBS, a conference consists of a number of separate topics where each topic contains a number of threads, and each thread is a chain of related messages. A user can thus read the messages as if following the development of a conversation.

Conferencing

A generic term used to cover various types of system which link people together. The main variants are video conferencing, audio conferencing, audiographic conferencing and computer conferencing. All except the last link people together synchronously – that is, the people are present simultaneously, even if separated in space.

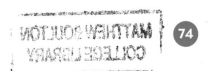

Dial-up
Connection to the Internet over an ordinary telephone line by dialling up a service provider's PoP.

Domain name system (DNS)
A domain is an individual network. The Internet is divided up into domains on a hierarchical basis. The domain name system maps Internet protocol addresses to individual computers within the domain. Internet e-mail addresses include domain name information.

Download
To obtain a file from another computer electronically. Downloaded information can then be displayed or saved to disk.

Digital data network
A network specifically designed for the transmission of data in digital form, eg ISDN, as distinct from analogue networks such as the telephone system.

EDI
Electronic data interchange: a system for exchanging database information in standardised form between computer systems, eg examination entries, personnel records.

Electronic mail (e-mail)
The electronic transmission and reception of information in asynchronous mode – that is, without the sender and recipient needing to be simultaneously present. Originally, electronic mail was text-based, and most systems on wide area networks are still restricted to text, but on local area networks modern electronic mail systems can transmit images, audio and even video messages (if the bandwidth is sufficient).

E-mail attachment
A file attached to an e-mail message carrying more complex information, eg a document with formatting codes, spreadsheet, graphic image, sound, video sequence.

Ethernet
A means of connecting computers in a local area network enabling rapid transfer of data (about 10Mb/sec) between machines over twisted pair cable or optical fibre.

Eudora
A popular e-mail reader for the Apple Macintosh and PC.

FAQ
Frequently-asked questions – a document that contains common questions and answers, usually on-line and posted to Usenet lists.

Fax modem
A type of modem which, in addition to its normal data transmission capabilities, handles fax. In conjunction with suitable software, a fax modem allows a microcomputer to operate like a fax machine, in the sense that any electronic document can be 'printed' to the fax modem and thus sent out as a fax. Some fax modems with suitable software allow the reception of faxes and their display on the computer screen.

Fibre optic cable
Very thin strands of pure glass, used for transmitting high volumes of data at high speed.

File library
An area on a BBS for storing files available to callers.

File transfer
Copying a file from one user to another.

Finger
An Internet application that can find information about a named user, for instance:
```
finger xx@company.ac.uk.
```

Firewall
A computer configured for security reasons to filter and control network traffic to and from the outside world.

FTP

File transfer protocol: a common method of transferring files from one computer to another over a TCP/IP network. Anonymous ftp is a way of copying files from an ftp server without having an account on the system in your name.

Gateway

A device connecting two different network systems by carrying out protocol conversion between them.

GIF

Graphics interchange format: digitised pictures are often stored and exchanged in this format, as most computer systems can cope with it.

Gopher

A way of publishing information and accessing it using a hierarchical menu-based system. You need a Gopher client to connect to a remote server and retrieve the files you request.

HTML

Hypertext mark-up language: a code used in documents to indicate how information is to be displayed on the World Wide Web. HTML files are read by a Web browser and it interprets codes about the format and size of text and where links to other files are to be placed.

Hotlink

An area of a document which, when the screen pointer is over it and clicked, tells the computer to go to another document or site.

Hotlist

A way of storing frequently visited locations on the WWW in a list to aid easy retrieval. Works in the same way as a bookmark.

Interface

Equipment that enables signals to pass from one system to another in a standard form so that different types of computer can handle them

Internet

The inter-communicating set of computer networks which, thanks to the common language of TCP/IP, form a world-wide 'meganetwork'.

ISP

Internet service provider: an organisation with a direct connection to the Internet that provides connections to other users to the Internet.

IRC

Internet relay chat: allows users world wide to 'talk' to each other by sending text messages to all participating users in real time.

ISDN

Integrated Services Digital Network: an internationally compatible high-speed network used for digital services like video conferencing and relatively fast Internet access.

JANET

Joint Academic NETwork: a data communications network linking all universities and other tertiary sector institutions in the UK and connected to similar networks in other European countries and the US. JANET is a component network of the Internet.

JPEG

A data compression standard designed by the Joint Photographics Experts Group to store digitised colour and black-and-white photographs.

Jughead

A searching tool for finding information on specific Gophers. Unlike Veronica, it only searches the menu items of a named Gopher. As with Veronica, you can use Boolean logic (such as *and*, *or*, *not*).

K–12

Kindergarten to 12th grade: the American primary and secondary sectors of education.

LAN

Local area network, such as the network of computers in a room or building.

Leased line

A permanent connection over the telephone network to, for example, a PoP; telephone charges are per line rather than per call made. Therefore, regardless of use, the costs are fixed and predictable.

List server

A method of supporting a conferencing system using e-mail. There is no permanent message storage in the conference system. Instead, a message posted to the conference is sent to the list server. The list server then copies the message to every subscriber on its list. Each subscriber finds a copy of all the new conference messages waiting in the mail.

Mbit/s

Million bits per second. Ethernet works at up to 10 Mbit/s.

MIME

Multipurpose Internet mail extensions: a standard for e-mail attachments on the Internet.

Modem

MOdulator-DEMulator: a device which translates digital signals into analogue signals so that data can be carried over ordinary telephone lines. Modems operate at different speeds depending on the model – speeds are normally in the range 300 bit/s to 28,800 bit/s.

MPEG

A standard drawn up by the Moving Photographic Experts Group for storing digitised video in compressed form.

NCSA

National Centre for Supercomputing Applications.

Newsgroup

A Usenet bulletin board topic such as films, recipes or education.

NNTP

Network news transport protocol: a method of retrieving a batch of articles from Usenet.

NREN

National Research and Education Network: the proposed broadband successor to the Internet in the US.

Packet switching

A data transmission method that breaks down a flow of data into smaller units called packets. These are individually addressed and routed through a network. Advanced countries have at least one publicly available packet-switching network.

PoP

Point of presence: a location and telephone number provided by an Internet service provider for local dial-up access to the Internet by users. The more PoPs in the country, the more likely you are to pay only local call rates.

POP

Post Office Protocol. POP2 and POP3 are e-mail standards.

PPP

Point-to-point protocol: permits interactive TCP/IP over telephone lines where Ethernet is not available, as if your computer were part of the host network. More sophisticated and more efficient than SLIP (*see below*).

Protocol

A set of rules governing information flow in a communication system. Sometimes called 'data link control'.

PSTN

Public switched telephone network: the traditional analogue telephone network.

Routing

The selection of a communications path for the transmission of information from source to destination. A router is a piece of hardware connecting networks, for example a LAN to a WAN. Routers enable the networks on the Internet to communicate with each other and for messages to pass over it.

Server

In the context of the client–server model, a server is the software on a remote computer servicing the client with the resources the client requests.

SLIP
Serial line Internet protocol – permits interactive TCP/IP over telephone lines where Ethernet is not available, as if your computer were part of the host network. Simpler but slower than PPP.

SMTP
Simple mail transfer protocol: a standard on the Internet for electronic mail.

SuperJANET
The emerging broadband upgrade to the existing JANET network for high-speed data traffic, including video and voice. Most universities in the UK will be connected to SuperJANET by 1996.

TCP/IP
Transmission control protocol/Internet protocol: a collection of networking standards which underpin the Internet, enabling different computers to talk a common language.

Telnet
A protocol enabling a user to log on to other computers, usually over the Internet.

Terminal adaptor
Interface equipment between a computer and an ISDN line (the equivalent of a modem).

Upload
To send a file to a BBS.

URL
Uniform resource locator. A unique reference locating a file on the WWW, for instance:

`http://ncet.csv.warwick.ac.uk.`

Usenet
A world-wide news and message database.

Usenet newsgroup
A collection of Usenet messages on a single subject.

Veronica

A Veronica server maintains an index of Gopher servers and can be searched using any Gopher client. It returns results as a menu, so the resources can be reached directly by clicking on the desired filename.

WAIS

Wide area information service: a full text indexing tool for building keyword-searchable database servers.

Wide area network

As opposed to a local area network, which links computers at the same site, a WAN links computers over a large geographical area.

World Wide Web

Also known as the WWW, W3 or simply the Web. A distributed information service based around on-line hypertext documents accessed using a Web browser like Mosaic or Netscape. The system was developed by an Englishman, Tim Berners-Lee, at CERN, Europe's centre for research into particle physics, in Switzerland.

X.25

An international standard for public packet switched networks.

X.400

An international standard for electronic mail.

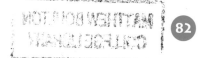

INTERNET SITES FOR EDUCATION

NOTES

- Details of these URLs were correct at the time of writing but they may change or be replaced.
- NCET has no control over the changes and inclusion here of a URL does not imply NCET endorsement.
- Enter them exactly as they appear here; do not use any spaces or carriage returns. If you are unsuccessful, try entering a shortened version – sometimes documents are relocated within the institution's internal filing system. For example:

  `http://galaxy.einet.net/`

  takes you higher up the site's directory structure than:

  `http://galaxy.einet.net/galaxy/Social Sciences/Education.html`.

- There are many other useful URLs, each of which could lead on to hundreds of others (there are around 2m); please let NCET and others know what you find.
- Several sites require browsers that have 'forms' facilities and/or particular graphical/audio viewers; other sites are specific to Mac or PC.
- Some sites contain large graphics and sound files which may cause your machine to 'freeze up'. Others may be inaccessible because of congestion, or simply because the computer is switched off.
- Unless otherwise stated, servers are American.

USEFUL STARTING POINTS FOR SUBJECT-RELATED INFORMATION

NCET (UK)

`http://ncet.csv.warwick.ac.uk/`

The NCET server contains information about all aspects of IT, together with an electronic version of its catalogue and a research and development area (where *Highways for Learning* is to be found). It

includes hotlinks to some of the servers listed here. It is regularly updated, so check it for recent information.

BBC Web Server (UK)

http://www.bbcnc.org.uk/
News of BBC programmes and support materials for educational broadcasts and a growing number of hotlinks to servers relevant to the UK national curriculum. Fact sheets and transcripts of parts of such programmes as the Big Byte are available. These are regularly updated and there is an archive feature which allows you to link to previously featured material. Do not confuse this open-access Web server with the BBC Networking Club – a subscription service.

The World Wide Web Virtual Library: Subject Catalogue (Switzerland)

http://info.cern.ch/hypertext/DataSources/bySubject/Overview.html
One of the most useful servers in any search for information.

World Wide Web Servers: Summary (Switzerland)

http://info.cern.ch/hypertext/DataSources/WWW/Servers.html
CERN is the home of the Web and this is where they try to keep track of all sites.

Schools Gophers (UK)

gopher://gopher.bham.ac.uk/11/edgophers
A rich source of curriculum-related materials from USA and Canada – including Schoolnet and KidLink.

Rice University

gopher://riceinfo.rice.edu/11/Subject
A good starting point for hotlinks to information by subject area. Also contains pointers to practically all K–12 resources. Directories contain links to resources organised by subject matter. The resources themselves are scattered all over the Internet. The selection of resources is based on several similar collections of such links maintained on a number of Gopher servers. Once a week the university runs a program which automatically merges selected directories of links at these institutions into the menus you see.

EINet Galaxy
`http://galaxy.einet.net/`
Another one-stop shop grouping large numbers of hotlinks to other servers under general headings such as leisure, education and politics. It also provides free access to the latest versions of its Macintosh and Windows Web client software (MacWeb and WinWeb). This site is echoed by other servers like http://www.gold.net, Goldsite Europe, probably Europe's busiest commercial Web server including the electronic magazines *Information Highway* and *On-Line Guardian*.

`http://galaxy.einet.net/galaxy/`
`Social-Sciences/Education.html`
A sub-section of the above, this provides a directory of education resources including US academic institutions, K–12 links, a US Department of Education link plus Edupage newsletter – a thrice-weekly newsletter of IT information provided by the University of Surrey from electronic mail received from the US (http://www.ee.surrey.ac.uk/edupage/).

Web servers by Country (Italy)
`http://hp133.na.infn.it/links/links.html`
Useful for tracking down Web servers country by country.

Ultralab (UK)
`http://www.ultralab.anglia.ac.uk/`
A UK server showing imaginatively the potential of the Internet.

World ORT Union (UK)
`http://www.ort.org/`
This UK educational server has been recently established by the IT department within the World ORT Union, an educational charity operating in more than 50 countries.

Encyclopedia Britannica on-line
`http://www.eb.com/`
A tempting glimpse of the on-line encyclopedia – as long as your search is restricted to A to C. The other letters are available via password to subscribers only.

Global Network Navigator

http://www.gnn.com/gnn/gnn.html

Carefully organised links to a host of useful places around the
Internet. Of particular note is the regularly updated 'What's new?'
section. Other features include Digital Drive-in (a section about
movies on the Internet) and NetNews (a weekly round-up of Internet
news).

Library of Congress World Wide Web Home Page

http://lcweb.loc.gov/

Many resources of this vast library are now available over the
Internet.

Cisco Educational Archive and Resources Catalog

http://sunsite.unc.edu/cisco/edu-arch.html

A well organised and selective catalogue of American educational
resources. There is a section encouraging institutions to create and
maintain information pages at no cost.

The Ask ERIC Virtual Library

http://ericir.syr.edu/

The Educational Resources Information Center (ERIC) provides
access to an extensive body of education-related literature and various
services and products at all education levels. AskERIC is an Internet-
based question-answering service for teachers, library media specialists, and administrators. Anyone involved with K–12 education can
send an e-mail message to askeric@ericir.syr.edu. Drawing on the
extensive resources of the ERIC system, AskERIC staff will respond
with an answer within 48 working hours.

POST-SCHOOLS SERVERS

Educational Technology Information and Resources (UK)

http://www.csv.warwick.ac.uk/WWW/hefc/

Edu-Tech holds information about HEFC initiatives such as the
Computers in Teaching Initiative (CTI) and the Teaching and
Learning Technology Project (TLTP), together with details of relevant workshops and conferences. Edu-Tech is a starting point for discovering what expertise, support and teaching materials are freely
available. For example, the CTI represents 20 subject centres, each

working within its own discipline to provide information on using technology in teaching and learning. All centres produce regular newsletters and software compendia, run workshops and open days, and answer subject-specific enquiries. Likewise, TLTP encompasses over 70 projects (institutional and consortium-based) mainly engaged in the production of technology-based materials for undergraduate courses. Members of an HEFC-funded university are entitled to use the CTI centres and to receive newsletters and resource directories.

National Information Services and Systems (UK)

`gopher://gopher.niss.ac.uk/`

Wide-ranging information for HE including bulletin board data plus education and research papers and reports from the committees within the UK higher education community.

JANET Information WWW Server (UK)

`http://www.jnt.ac.uk/`

The Joint Academic NETwork links UK universities with each other and the world. The server holds information about JANET, the United Kingdom's academic and research network. A 'What's new' section contains details of recent additions to the server, together with further information being available on specific topics. A liaison desk is the main point of contact for enquiries about JANET services and requests for information. The liaison desk staff deal with applications to connect to JANET and also process upgrade requests for existing connections.

Leicester University

`http://www.cs.ucl.ac.uk/misc/uk/leicester.html`

An example of a university's server; a good way for prospective students to get a feel for university life without spending a day out of school.

TEACHER EDUCATION

ITTI Home Page (UK)

`http://www.hull.ac.uk/Hull/ITTI/itti.html`

A server for the IT in Teaching Initiative, which has funded 29 projects in UK universities. These include IT skills training (such as geographic information systems, statistics and graphics), multimedia

and hypertext courseware development tools and training, professional IT skills training for UNIX, X-Windows and networking.

Teacher Education Internet Server
gopher://state.virginia.edu/
An American server providing documents related to professional
development.

American Association of Teachers of French
gopher://utsainfo.utsa.edu:7070/1
An example of what could develop in Europe – a subject association
which networks teachers and provides added value for members.

The Edweb Project
http://edweb.cnidr.org:90
EdWeb, including the K–12 Internet Guide, allows you to explore on-
line educational resources around the world, learn about trends in
education reform, examine success stories of computers in the classroom, and much more. Numerous changes and additions every day.

Cisco educational archives
http://sunsite.unc.edu/cisco/
tracy-article.html
Here you will find the paper describing the Internet for US schools
which is summarised in Chapter 5.

ENGLISH

The *Electronic Telegraph* (UK)
http://www.telegraph.co.uk/Register.html
The *Daily Telegraph* on the Internet. You will need to register your
name and e-mail number and remember an eight-digit PIN number.

The *Guardian* (UK)
http://www.gold.net/online/
Back copies of the 'On-Line' section of the *Guardian*.

Buena Vista Press Room
http://bvp.wdp.com:80/BVPM/MooVPlex.html
Film materials from Walt Disney, including synopses and video clips
of 101 Dalmations.

Gutenberg server

http://www.med.ansa.bu.ed

Two thousand out-of-copyright texts.

Purdue On-Line Writing Lab

http://owl.trc.purdue.edu//

The OWL Web offers a variety of writing-related information in an interesting and attractive format. The Owl Web offers lists of writing material on the Internet, other writing labs on the Internet and places to start your Internet-based research.

Poetry at Carnegie Mellon University

http://english-server.hss.cmu.edu/Poetry.html

MATHEMATICS

MegaMath Project

http://www.c3.lanl.gov/mega-math/welcome.html

The MegaMath project is intended to bring unusual and important mathematical ideas (for example, the concept of infinity) to elementary school classrooms so that young people and their teachers can think about them together.

Learning Multiplication Tables

gopher://ericir.syr.edu/00/Lesson/Math/
cecmath.02

An example from the K–12 initiative of how the Internet can help teachers share ideas.

Shell Centre for Mathematical Education (UK)

http://acorn.edu.nottingham.ac.uk/ShellCent/

CSC Mathematical Topics

http://www.csc.fi/math_topics/General.html

The Center for Scientific Computing provides information, links to other maths-related servers and keyword search facilities.

A Gallery of Interactive On-Line Geometry

http://www.geom.umn.edu/apps/gallery.html

Helps students to apply geometrical theory to pictures they themselves create.

SCIENCE

Natural History Museum (UK)

http://www.nhm.ac.uk/

One of the first UK museums to set up an Internet server. Information
on the museum's exhibitions, public programmes, the museum's
work and its collections.

Smithsonian Natural History Museum

http://nmnhwww.si.edu/nmnhweb.html

An American museum offering similar information.

NetSpace Project

http://netspace.students.brown.edu/

Brown University NetSpace Project is a student-run organisation; this
server includes information about the project and students' hotlists.

Earth and Environmental Science

http://info.er.usgs.gov/network/science/
earth/index.html

The US Geological Survey's server.

NASA Information Services via World Wide Web

http://nasa.gov/

This includes details of all NASA educational resources together with
a 'sensitive' map of the USA which gives easy access to 13 major
NASA sites.

Enviroweb

http://envirolink.org

The largest on-line environmental information service.

Virtual Frog Dissection

http://curry.edschool.Virginia.EDU:80/
~insttech/frog/
http://george.lbl.gov/ITG.hm.pg.docs/
dissect/info.html

Two Web sites introduce you to the intricacies of frog dissection –
while one concentrates on the parts of the frog, the other is an on-line
tutorial.

SeaWorld and Busch Gardens Information Database

`http://www.bev.net:80/education/SeaWorld`

Sea World and Busch Gardens provide an imaginative and intellectually stimulating atmosphere for students. Features include Animal Bytes – designed to find information about some of the creatures found in the animal kingdom. Each file includes their scientific classification, fun facts, and biological value.

TECHNOLOGY

`http://web.cnam.fr/Images/Usenet/abpm/summaries/`

Its purpose is to help you to select and retrieve files distributed on the news. You can read a description file or you can choose a contact sheet, a map file and click on the image you prefer.

MODERN LANGUAGES

The Human Languages Page

`http://www.willamette.edu/~tjones/Language-Page.html`

A–Z resource list of foreign language-related information on the Net; first stop for the linguist.

CTI Centre for Modern Languages (UK)

`gopher://gopher.hull.ac.uk/11/cti`

Hull University is the home of this national modern languages project for higher education; archives of ReCall journal are available here, together with useful reviews of software.

Revue quotidienne de la presse en France (France)

`gopher://avril.ambaottawa.fr/00/rep3/rep34/rep346/menu3464.txt`

A daily digest of the French press, for advanced linguists.

German News, Jahresübersicht (Germany)

`http://www.rz.uni-karlsruhe.de/misc/germnews/`

A similar service for German speakers.

Les serveurs W3 en France (France)
http://web.urec.fr/france/france.html
All the Web servers based in France; other countries' servers can be
found at Servers of the World:
http://info.cern.ch/hypertext/DataSources/
WWW/Servers.html

Association des Bibliophiles Universels (France)
http://www.cnam.fr/ABU/principal/ABU.v2.html
A resource bank of French language texts.

Grenoble (France)
http://www.grenet.fr/gid/
An attractive and informative server well worth a visit.

Paris (France)
http://www.urec.fr/France/Paris.html
http://meteora.ucsd.edu/~norman/paris/
Two Web sites about Paris, including an on-line métro route-finder.
American English predominates.

Ministère de la culture et de la francophonie (France)
http://www.culture.fr/
Information about French museums and art galleries.

Elementary Spanish
http://www.cyborganic.com/~lesliev/Curriculum/
A complete Spanish curriculum.

HISTORY

Jesuits and Sciences 1600–1800
http://www.luc.edu/~scilib/jessci.html
Collection of texts and images from rare works on astronomy,
cosmology, engineering, mathematics and national history.

The Commonwealth of Learning (Canada)

http://www.col.org/

This server is maintained by the Commonwealth of Learning based in Vancouver, Canada. It includes facts, figures and statistics on all the Commonwealth countries and aims to create and widen access to education and to improve its quality, utilising distance education techniques and associated communications technologies to meet the particular requirements of member countries.

Volcano World

http://volcano.und.nodak.edu

Volcano World is funded by NASA specifically to provide information about volcanoes to school children. Includes photos, information and a developing virtual field trip to Kilauea volcano.

Planet Earth Home Page

http://white.nosc.mil/info.html

Includes a wide selection of information including items on world regions, community, sciences and information sources.

Japan 2000 Japanese Information (Japan)

http://http://www.ntt.jp:80/japan/

Puerto Rico

http://hppprdk01.prd.hp.com/

Facts, history, places to visit, beautiful images.

ART

Le WebLouvre (France)

http://mistral.enst.fr/~pioch/louvre/louvre.html

Voted the best Web site in 1994.

OTIS (Operative Term Is Stimulate)

http://sunsite.unc.edu/otis/art-links.html

Details of over 46 art-related servers from around the globe.

MUSIC

Music Web servers

http://www.galcit.caltech.edu/~ta/mtv/
musicpages.html

Planet Starchild

http://www.mcs.com/~bliss/starchild/home.html

Indie musicbox – new music from across the globe together with
links to music utilities that can be downloaded, on-line multimedia
and sound catalogues.

Music resources

http://www.cecer.army.mil/burnett/MDB/
musicResources.html

A detailed source to music servers: Rock band servers – 99 of them,
from Pink Floyd to ZZTop and including the Rolling Stones but not
Cliff Richard; 13 different styles of music with samples to download;
plus 54 miscellaneous reference sites, from Leeds University
Department of Music (details of concert schedules, events) to the
Hype Electrazine.

New Zealand Symphony Orchestra (New Zealand)

http://actrix.gen.nz/users/dgold/nzso.html

Classical music around New Zealand: schedule of events, links to
many world classical music resources on the WWW.

The Rolling Stones

http://www.stones.com/

From where the first Internet live concert was 'multicast' in
November 1994. You can download the 2.5 Mb 'Sympathy for the
Devil', but it may take more than 45 minutes.

OTHER SITES WORTH A VISIT

Greenpeace International

http://www.cyberstore.ca/greenpeace/index.html

Gives the Greenpeace view of current environmental concerns:
atmosphere, ozone and ocean ecology.

Veggies Unite!

`http://jalapeno.ucs.indiana.edu/`
`cgi-bin/recipes/`

The one-stop shop for vegetarians – a searchable index of over 1500 vegetarian recipes.

Hungerweb

`http://www.hunger.brown.edu/hungerweb`

Part of Browns University server, Indiana, USA, that deals with topical issues of famine and the crisis in Rwanda – radio broadcasts can be downloaded; international document transcripts are available; a variety of maps of the area can be viewed and downloaded. It includes an interactive quiz with on-line feedback, together with the opportunity to mail directly the US President.

Welcome to the White House

`http://www.whitehouse.gov/White_House/html/`
`White_House_Home-plain.html`

An interactive citizen's handbook, this URL has a text interface. For the full graphical representation type http://www.whitehouse.gov/

Treasury (UK)

`http://www.hm-treasury.gov.uk`

The first UK ministry to have its own Web server. It includes long lists of ministers' speeches and treasury news reports.

CCTA Government Information Service (UK)

`http://www.open.gov.uk/`

A UK open-government initiative in support of the Citizen's Charter. Information sources include HMSO, the Office of Public Service and Science, and the Citizen's Charter Unit.

I'M Europe (Luxembourg)

`http://www.echo.lu`

Ever wanted the full text of the Maastricht treaty? Look no further. I'M Europe is an initiative of Directorate-General XIII of the EC to provide the World Wide Web with information about Europe and the European electronic information market.

Cyberia café (UK)

http://www.easynet.co.uk/pages/cafe/cafe.htm

The Net pages of the first Internet cafe (in London) where you can buy a coffee and surf the Net at a charged half-hourly rate. Includes good links to other pages.

SITES ABOUT THE INTERNET

URouLette wheel

http://www.cen.uiuc.edu/cgi-bin/ryl

If you connect to this URL it randomly selects a server related to education and connects you to it – a good, if haphazard, way of appreciating the sheer amount of information available.

BoWeb '94 Award Recipients

http://wings.buffalo.edu/contest/awards/
index.html

Listings and hotlinks for the best Web sites in 1994 as voted by Internet users.

Human Computer Interface Research

www.hydra.bgsu.edu

Internet and Comms Today (UK)

http://www.gpl.net/customers/ict/ict.html

The contents list and selected articles from current and previous issues of this new magazine.

Fuse

http://www.worldserver.pipex.com/fuse94/

This is an interactive magazine (available on subscription) that sets out to challenge current ideas about typography and visual language in an age of ever-changing communications technologies.

Microsoft Home Page

http://www.microsoft.com/pages/services/
msnet/msnintro.htm

Internet Training Resources on the Web

http://www.brandonu.ca/~ennsnr/resources.html

This collection includes links to over 50 training resources. Included are pointers to the December, Yanoff and Awesome lists, the Network Training Materials Gopher, many guides to the Internet and mailing lists.

Online Dictionary of Computing (FOLDOC)

http://wombat.doc.ic.ac.uk

A searchable dictionary of everything to do with computing.

SEARCHING THE WEB – A SELECTION OF TOOLS

Lycos

http://lycos.cs.cmu.edu/

Enables fast searches (seconds rather than minutes) to take place across the 1.85 million unique URLs on the WWW. You can search both titles and content simply by typing in a word. Lycos will also make some decisions about which finds to list for you based on frequency of the search words. Access is often denied when too many people are trying to use it.

WorldWideWebWorm

http://www.cs.colorado.edu/home/mcbryan/WWWW.html

This was voted best navigational aid in 1994. Fairly close to comprehensive and very popular. The WWW Worm is a robot which indexes titles, URLs, and reference links.

Using Galaxy

http://www.galaxy.einet.net/search.htm

Searching for Software on WWW

http://src.doc.ic.ac.uk/archieplexform.html

SunSITE Northern Europe (UK)

http://src.doc.ic.ac.uk

PUBLISHING ON THE WEB

Creating Web servers
http://learning.lib.vt.edu/webserv/webserv.html
An excellent introduction to educational uses of the Web and to why and how everyone should set up their own.

The Learned InfoNet
http://info.learned.co.uk/
Learned Information Ltd publishes an extensive range of books, conference proceedings, newspapers, newsletters and learned journals for both providers and users of information in many industry sectors. The company also acts as learned publisher/distributor for many industry associations and societies, including the UK On-line User Group.

Harry M. Kriz
http://learning.lib.vt.edu/authors/hmkriz.html
An example of an individual's home page. Harry M. Kriz has a variable page called Page o' the Day where links change irregularly. At the time of writing there is a link to a German server which has the full version of *Alice's Adventures in Wonderland* and *Through the Looking Glass*, complete with the illustrations.

Hillside Elementary School
http://hillside.coled.umn.edu/
One of the growing number of schools running their own Web servers, complete with pages created by pupils and their individual Internet address (not an idea to copy).

Low Bentham County Primary School Web Page
http://cres1.lancs.ac.uk/~esarie/school.htm
One of the first UK schools' Web pages on a UK server; includes the school prospectus, Kirsten's drawing of the school and a photograph of typical Karst scenery.

Langley Junior and Infant School
http://www-bprc.mps.ohio-state.edu/
cgi-bin/hpp/langleyji.html

Hinchingbrooke Secondary School
http://www.bbcnc.org.uk/online/schools/
hinchhome.html

Scottish Highlands and Islands server (UK)

`http://nsa.bt.co.uk/nsa.html`

A server illustrating how the Internet can serve isolated communities and keep people in touch in new ways.

Web server shareware

`http//www.emwac.ac.uk`

Edinburgh University Computing Service have developed shareware versions of Gopher and Web servers for Windows NT enabling you to set up a server in less than four minutes, they claim. The software is included on the Microsoft Windows NT Resource Kit and is available via FTP from this site.

0410–001/03–95/5K/CP